TRUSTING GOD IN TROUBLED TIMES

*Daily Breakfasts
With the Master*

by

Carol Hopson

TABLE OF CONTENTS

iv

PREFACE

Trusting God in Troubled Times

This morning a very unusual thing happened at our house; we lost our electricity. For some of you that may not be rare, but I assure you it doesn't happen very often in San Diego County, so we were caught off guard. We were totally without power and light, and it changed everything! I suddenly realized that I couldn't get ready because it was too dark to put my makeup on in my bathroom. I couldn't cook, I couldn't work on my computer or study for upcoming retreats, I couldn't read or do anything I needed to do...all because there was no light or power.

This happened just as I was beginning to write this book. As my husband and I went out to take a walk in the dark morning, God began speaking to my heart, and He overwhelmed me with this thought: "Look at all the things you can't do because of the loss of power and light! It's the same in your spiritual life. Without beginning your day with Me, you have no power or light for your day." I realized that when I'm not **feasting on His Word** for my daily nourishment, I begin focusing on what is going on around me...the financial state of our country, the political situation, personal problems, and so on.

Then, as God so often lovingly leads me, He prompted me to write about the importance of having "**breakfast**

with Him" each morning so that we will be prepared, nourished, and ready for whatever our day brings. So this devotional book is about beginning your day at the breakfast table that our precious Savior has prepared for us. **It's about learning to trust Him in these troubled times**! It will then be your responsibility to "**come and dine**" and receive the nourishment He offers. I encourage you not to miss a single "breakfast" with Him as He has so much to offer.

My Power and Light

I never should begin my day
Without Your mighty power.
I need Your help so much, dear Lord,
For every single hour.

I've tried to go about my day
Without time in Your Word,
And it just leaves me frustrated
And I have no reserve.

But when I start my day with You,
I'm able to believe
That all that happens in my day,
You'll help me to receive.

For with your light and power in me,
I will not bring You shame,
I'll know that all things can work out
To glorify Your name.

-Carol Hopson

BREAKFAST #1

Preparing the meal...

HOW TO DELIGHT IN GOD'S WORD

Thou hast ordained Thy precepts, that we should keep them diligently....I will meditate on Thy precepts, and regard Thy ways. I shall delight in Thy statutes; I shall not forget Thy word.
-Psalm 119:4, 15-16

My husband was on a mission trip to Russia and was invited to share his Christian morals and values with public school educators. As they gathered in a large circle in the sparse room, he noticed there was no place to set his notes and Bible as all of the seats were filled, and he was in a chair also. Before he began, he set his binder and Bible on the floor beneath his chair, and someone immediately raced over to pick it up and hand it to him. You see, this dear person had such respect for God's precious Word that she couldn't let it sit on the floor, even for a moment. We don't even know if she was a believer.

I have also heard of believers in third world countries who didn't have a Bible, but they found a box that a Bible came in and treasured the box because it once contained the Holy Word of God. Oh, how far we've come from that respect in our country. I love shopping at thrift stores, and I often see used, discarded Bibles in all stages of neglect. They are usually near the floor and are very dusty. I also notice that few people take their Bibles to church any more, and I rarely see anyone carrying one at all.

I wonder what would happen if we treated our Bibles as we treat our cell phones?

- What if we carried it everywhere in our purses or pockets?

- What if we turned back to get it if we forgot it?

- What if we felt totally lost without checking it several times a day?

- What if we treated it as if we couldn't live without it?

- What if we checked regularly for messages and responded promptly to them?

- What if we gave it to kids and friends as gifts?

- What if we used it in case of an emergency?

Does that give you a little food for thought? It really gets to my heart. How have we lost sight of the significance and treasure that we have in God's Word? I think we have taken our freedom to own, study, and memorize God's Word for granted so long that it no longer even seems special to us, and so we are fretting about these troubled times rather than feasting on God's Word for peace. I once heard a speaker, who was from Communist Bulgaria, at an Association of Christian Schools International Convention. Her family was one of the few Christian families in that country, and she knew the Lord from an early age. Her father was a pastor in Bulgaria and was martyred for his faith when she was a young girl. Her mother and brother were also killed for their Christian faith, but somehow she survived.

Years later, after winning a European violin competition, she was officially assigned to work in East Germany as a concert violinist. But because of her faith, she was forced to make a dramatic escape to the United States in 1982. In sharing her testimony, she told us that all of the Bibles had been destroyed in Bulgaria as the government officials went around to all of the churches and homes and confiscated them. However, one brave lady sat on hers, tucking her clothing around it while sitting through the search of their church. It was the only remaining Bible in their city that they knew of.

When it was safe enough, the congregation met at the little church and wondered what they would do without their precious Bibles. This one woman, with tear-filled eyes, began tearing out page after page of her Bible. As she did this, she handed one to every person there so that each believer could have a page of God's Word. For twenty-five years, this woman, who was speaking to us, had only one page of God's Word...Genesis 16 and 17. As she held that one well-worn, tear-stained page up for us to see, I couldn't stop the tears from streaming down my face. How could I take having all of God's Word so lightly? Do I really believe that it is "*a lamp to my feet, and a light to my path*" (Psalm 119:105)? Or can I really say that,

> *Thy testimonies are wonderful; therefore my soul observes them. The unfolding of Thy words gives light; it gives understanding to the simple.*
> (Psalm 119:129)

This dear child of God said that the one thing she prayed for all those years, and the one thing she desired when she came to America, was to have a whole Bible.

I have never forgotten that woman or her story. Because of hearing it, I have sought to treasure God's Word more and spend more time studying, obeying, and memorizing it...especially as I look at the world around me. What a difference it has made in my life! "*Thy testimonies are the joy of my heart*" (Psalm 119:111). "*Establish Thy word to Thy servant, as that which produces reverence for Thee*" (Psalm 119:38). I pray that as you go through this devotional book, you will develop more reverence and love for your Savior and His love letter to you! This then will be the key to trusting in troubled times!

GOD'S PRECIOUS WORD

The Word of God meets all my needs
And feeds my hungry soul.
It helps me know just how to live
And identifies my role.

Sometimes it seems so difficult
To see what I must do,
But with God's loving grace and help
He'll always see me through.

For all I truly need to know
About this life of mine
Is found within this tear-stained Book,
God's precious Word divine!

-Carol Hopson

COME AND DINE...

1. Do you think you need to improve in how you handle God's Word? If you've taken the privilege of having His Word for granted, why not pray and ask God to help you truly learn to treasure His precious Word.

2. Look again at "what if we treated our Bibles like we treat our cell phones." Write out two or three ways that you might try to use your Bible more for direction and victory in your daily life.

3. Feast on Psalm 119:129-160, and write out all the benefits of studying God's Word that you find.

4. Which ones do you need the most right now in these troubled times, and what will you do about it?

Either God's Word will keep you from sin,
or sin will keep you from God's Word.

BREAKFAST #2

Preparing the meal...

REMEMBER THAT GOD IS IN CONTROL!

Cast your burden upon the LORD, and He will sustain you; He will never allow the righteous to be shaken.

-Psalm 55:22

Humble yourselves, therefore, under the mighty hand of God, that He may exalt you at the proper time, casting all your anxiety upon Him, because He cares for you.

-1 Peter 5:6-7

I was just about ready to have a large, formal Christmas dinner at my house. I was calling it an "Encouragement Dinner" because so many people we loved and cared about were going through very difficult times. Some had financial hardships, some had hurtful work-related problems, and still others had devastating family issues. I was thrilled to be able to invite these dear friends into our home so that we could share some Scripture passages with them, encourage them, and pray for them.

About one hour before they were to arrive, I received a very upsetting phone call, and there was nothing I could do about the situation. As I hung up the phone, I asked the Lord why He would have me receive that very difficult news right before I was trying to encourage so many people...and just when I was so busy and had so much still to do before they arrived. God's timing seemed to be all off in my opinion. But I knew that was wrong thinking, and it didn't go along with what I knew from God's Word, so I had to quickly call on God to help me change my thinking.

I sat down and began asking God for calmness, peace, and direction from His Word. And as I sat there, God revealed some very important, wonderful things to me. First of all, He whispered to me that He knew all about this situation...it wasn't a surprise to Him. That was so comforting to me to realize that! God hadn't lost control; He knew about this situation before the call came to me. Secondly, He knew I would hear that news just before the dinner, and therefore it must have been for my good.

We know that God causes all things to work together for good to those who love God.
Romans 8:28

Thirdly, He knew that it would be a great concern to me, and yet it had passed through His will. All of these gave me instant comfort, but then He showed me what He wanted me to do with what He had just revealed to me. Here are the four things He poured into my heart that day...while dinner was waiting...while guests were on their way...while much still needed to be done...but while my heart was seeking His peace.

Yes, God knew all about this problem, He knew I would hear it at this specific time, and He knew it would greatly concern me. However...

1. **He still wanted me to cast all my worries on Him!**

Cast your burden upon the Lord, and He will sustain you.

-Psalm 55:22

The word cast in Psalm 55:22 refers to actually "rolling off" the heavy weight of the burden onto Jesus. I pictured having a steamroller on my chest as the burden felt so heavy. Then I pictured rolling it down off of my chest, down over my body, all the way down and off my feet, leaving it at Jesus' feet. Wow! That felt incredibly good!

2. **He still wanted me to delight to do His will**!
Psalm 40:8 says,

I delight to do Thy will, O my God. Thy Law is within my heart.

For victory at this moment, I needed to delight in obeying God, in giving my burden to Him, in letting Him take control of my thoughts, and in continuing to reach out to encourage others. In delighting to do His will, it took my thoughts off of myself and my problems and put my focus back on serving the Lord.

3. **He still wanted me to trust Him completely!**

Trust in the LORD with all your heart, and do not lean on your own understanding. In all your ways acknowledge Him, and He will make your paths straight.

-Proverbs 3:5-6

To obey these verses meant that I wouldn't fret about what I heard, doubt that He was able to work out His plan, or feel heavy-hearted with the burden. If I truly trusted Him with ALL my heart, I could leave it all with Him and walk on in peace.

4. **He still wanted me to obey His words so my steps would not slip**! Psalm 37:31 says,

The law of his God is in his heart; his steps do not slip.

The previous verse tells us that this is speaking of a righteous person who is right before God. What words from God's law could I think of to keep me from slipping into worry or fear? Here are two verses that God immediately brought to my mind:

No soldier in active service entangles himself in the affairs of everyday life, so that he may please the one who enlisted him as a soldier.
-2 Timothy 2:4

The battle is not yours but God's...stand and see the salvation of the LORD on your behalf.
-2 Chronicles 20:15, 17

Yes, Lord! I will obey Your Word and be Your servant as I love and serve those whom You are bringing into my home for encouragement tonight. Thank You for calming my heart and giving me a perfect example of Your light, power, and love to share with these dear friends tonight! Amen.

COME AND DINE...

1. Do you remember the last time you were anxious or fearful over some news you heard or what you read in the paper or saw on the TV? Write down how you felt.

2. Now that you've gone through this lesson, what can you do the next time you are faced with discouraging, troubling, or difficult news?

3. Feast on 2 Chronicles 20:1-30 and answer the following questions:

What caused Jehoshaphat to be fearful?

What did he do with His fear? List several choices he made and the verses that show these choices.

What truths did he focus on that kept him from panic?

What did God do for Jehoshaphat?

> *We all have crosses to bear, but let us not forget that it depends on the spirit in which we bear the cross as to whether it becomes an agony or a glory.*
> -Cliff Cole

BREAKFAST #3

Preparing the meal...

DO YOU NEED SOMEONE TO CARE?

I am Alpha and Omega, the beginning and the ending, saith the Lord, which is, and which was, and which is to come, the Almighty [El Shaddai].
-Revelation 1:8, KJV

Have there been times in your life when you asked, "Does anyone care what I'm going through?" I've certainly felt that way, especially when I didn't understand what God was doing or allowing in my life. I knew God was mighty and powerful, but did He care about my concerns? When Abraham was ninety-nine years old, he needed reassurance from God as to what He had promised him when he was seventy-five years old. God had promised that he would have a son and that his descendants would be as the stars (Genesis 15:4-5). Abraham had waited twenty-four years for this promise to be fulfilled, yet nothing had changed. Now he and Sarah were past the child-bearing age.

God cared about Abraham's concern, and so He appeared to him and spoke these words: "*I am the Almighty*

God [El Shaddai]; walk before me, and be thou perfect" (Genesis 17:1, KJV). This was the first time God revealed this part of His character, and it meant that He was strong enough to help Abraham, yet sensitive enough to care about him. This name also implied that God could supply all his needs while being both strong and tender. Just a week ago I was talking with a young woman who had rejected God because she was raised in a church where she only heard about God's condemnation and judgment; she never heard about His love and genuine concern for His children. I tried to explain to her the "Shepherd's heart" of our God, and she had a very difficult time believing that because she only knew of God's wrath.

I heard a wonderful illustration of this aspect of El Shaddai when I received a phone call one day from another state. The pleasant male voice asked if I was the Carol Hopson who had written *But God, This Wasn't My Plan!* and *But God, I'm Tired of Waiting*. I responded that I was, and then he told me an amazing story of God's tender care. He said that God had moved him and his wife to another state to serve as pastor in a church there. They had prayed much and had left a church they dearly loved in obedience to the Lord. (I could identify with this man already!) He then went on to explain all the pain, loneliness, and defeat they had both experienced in the past nine months. He also said that his wife was in a deep depression and he didn't know where to turn or what to do. He was just asking God to help him as his wife walked upstairs to lie down on their bed. In a few minutes, she returned and asked, "Do you know where these two books came from?" He looked at them and replied, "No." She then told him that they were lying in plain sight. She had never seen them before and couldn't remember if someone had given them to her or what. He looked at the titles in total amazement and told his wife that maybe God had heard their cry.

So they sat down together and began reading *But God, This Wasn't My Plan*! He said they wept so many tears and that God spoke so clearly to them about how they had gotten off track spiritually. As they finished the second book, they both confessed their anger, fear, and doubt to the Lord and then recommitted this new ministry to the Lord and promised to walk on with faith in His plan, not theirs. His call was one of victorious thanks and praise to our God for caring so deeply for them that He somehow put these two books in their hands.

That's exactly who El Shaddai is! Do you need El Shaddai today? He doesn't promise to remove our mountains or valleys, but He promises to give us His strength and power to endure whatever He allows. He promises to walk beside us and tenderly care for us along the way. "*For I am the LORD your God, who upholds your right hand, who says to you, 'Do not fear, I will help you'*" (Isaiah 41:13). And He promises to use us for His glory if we allow Him to (Psalms 40:1-3). In his book called My Father's Names, Elmer L. Towns gives us some guidelines to help us overcome our problems as we understand more about El Shaddai.

1. **Separate yourself from sin**. "*Many of our problems come because of sin in our lives. It is the nature of sin to defeat, destroy, disrupt, dilute and damage the child of God.*" If we harbor sin in our lives, He must judge and cannot be merely tender and kind (2

Corinthians 6:17-18). When you're feeling distraught or fearful, pray the prayer of David in Psalm 139:23-24: *"Search me, O God, and know my heart; try me and know my anxious thoughts; and see if there be any hurtful way in me, and lead me in the everlasting way."*

2. **Rest in the presence of El Shaddai**. Sheep only truly rest from conflict and fear when their shepherd is present because they know that he loves them, cares for them, and will lay down his life for them if necessary. Adrian Rogers in his book entitled The Lord Is My Shepherd writes, "Every good shepherd knows how important it is to lead his sheep to places of rest because without his guidance, his sheep wouldn't choose to rest, and they probably wouldn't choose the greenest of pastures either. The Good Shepherd will make you lie down in green pastures, and He will lead you beside still waters if you trust Him with all your heart. The One who loves you and is compassionate, caring, and courageous" says, *"But when he saw the multitudes, he was moved with compassion on them, because they fainted, and were scattered abroad, as sheep having no shepherd."* Matthew 9:36 (KJV)

I think I can hear some of you asking, "But how does He make me lie down and rest?" That's a good question! In my experience, He uses various ways, such as an illness where I have to be still and listen, a prolonged trial or maybe a Scripture verse that stirs my heart to rest. Recently, the thing that has brought me to rest the most is realizing how stressed I can get thinking about problems with people, finances, or the daily news. And so, I am convicted by the Holy Spirit to find rest and comfort in focusing on El Shaddai, His love and care, the truths of His Word, and His constant presence with me. It always produces a restful heart.

3. **Carefully follow the directions of El Shaddai.** A child who is continually disobeying his parents is not in good standing with his parents. Likewise, we cannot be in fellowship with El Shaddai or feel His presence and tender care when we are not following His counsel. I think we so quickly forget warnings like this one: *"Be anxious for nothing, but in everything by prayer and supplication with thanksgiving let your requests be made known to God. And the peace of God, which sur-passes all comprehension, shall guard your hearts and your minds in Christ Jesus"* (Philippians 4:6-7). To know God's presence and peace in the valleys of life, we must willingly follow His directions.

COME AND DINE...

1. Have you experienced God as the One who tenderly cares for you? If not, read Psalm 23 and ask God to reveal Himself to you anew.

2. Are you waiting for God to answer a specific prayer right now? Write out the answer that you'd like to have, and then write out a prayer seeking God's answer to your need, rather than expecting your answer.

My desire:

Willing for God's desire:

3. Feast on Isaiah 55, and then answer the following:

Write down three things you learned about God in this passage.

What truths did you learn about God's Word?

What instructions were given for those who want to follow God?

The time I live in is a time of turmoil.
My hope is in God.
Frederick the Great, King of Prussia

BREAKFAST #4

Preparing the meal...

THE PURPOSE OF SURRENDER

Do you know that you are the temple of God, and that the Spirit of God dwells in you?...So then let no one boast in men, For all things belong to you...and you belong to Christ; and Christ belongs to God.
-1 Corinthians 3:16, 21, 23

Or do you not know that your body is a temple of the Holy Spirit who is in you, whom you have from God, and that you are not your own? For you have been bought with a price; therefore glorify God in your body.
-1 Corinthians 6:19-20

I was watching a popular TV evangelist interview a pastor from a very large church in a third world country. I had been to his country and was interested in what he was going to say. The TV evangelist asked the pastor what he thought of the Christians he had seen in the United States. He replied, "Well, they are pretty committed." The TV evangelist smiled and said, "That's good, isn't it?" The foreign pastor then said words I shall always remember. He responded, "Well, in America, I see Christians who are committed...but they choose what they will or will not be committed to. They choose to commit to God in some areas but not in others, and that's how they live. In my country, Christians do not just "commit, they surrender!" I wrote his words down as fast as I could so I would never forget them.

You see, commitment still gives control to the person, and they can decide if and when they want to be committed...maybe on Sunday...maybe when life is going well...maybe after they've been to Bible study...maybe in certain areas of their life but not all areas...and so on. But when you surrender, you have no control, no ownership, no choices...you belong to the one you surrendered to! Being a Christian means we surrender to the One who died for us. Think of war times, when a person or army surrenders, do they have control over what happens to them? Of course not...they are totally under the control and command of those they surrendered to. The difference is that we surrender to the One who loves us and gave His life for us, not to some terrible, frightening dictator.

This true account is from the book Extreme Devotion, published by the Voice of the Martyrs.

The pastor [from China] had been questioned and beaten often, but today the guard took him to a room to talk. He said, "I'm curious about your beliefs and ask you to tell me the Ten Commandments."

Shocked, the pastor began to share the commandments. When he got to "Honor your father and mother," the officer interrupted him. "Stop there. You Christians believe that God chose 'Honor your father and mother' as a very impor-

tant commandment. Please look in the corner." The pastor turned to see an elderly woman chained and bruised beneath a pile of rags. She was the pastor's own mother.

The guard inquired. "Look how much your mother has suffered. If you tell the secrets of the underground church, you and your mother can go free. If she dies from our torture, you will have failed to keep the commandment to honor her, and her blood shall be on your head."

The pastor turned to his mother who was starting to regain consciousness. "Dear Mother, what shall I do?"

Lovingly she replied, "Since you were a small boy, I have taught you to love Christ and his church. Do not betray God. I am ready to die for the holy name."

The pastor looked back at the guard and said with renewed courage, "You were very right, Captain. First of all, a man must obey his mother."

That was a picture of true surrender! I can't even imagine being in a situation like that. However, God gives us opportunities every day to make the choice to surrender to Him. So what does surrender look like in our daily lives?

- When we hear news that hurts or disturbs us, we choose to surrender the fear and pain to the Lord and ask Him to help us handle it in a way that honors Him.

- When we have a hard, frustrating day at work or at home with the kids, we surrender our selfish thoughts that tell us "you deserve better" and focus on God's love for us and our commitment to honor Him with our thoughts, words, and actions.

- When we hear that there might be an unwanted job

change or move, we surrender the future into God's hands and open our hearts to let Him work in us however He chooses.

● When we have repeated interruptions in our day and can't accomplish what we had planned or thought we needed to do, we surrender our plans and accept the changes as part of God's plan to mature us or His desire to give us new opportunities to show love and grace to others.

"I delight to do Thy will, O my God; Thy Law is within my heart" (Psalm 40:8). Surrender is really delighting to do God's will above my will...always and in all situations. He paid the price to have ALL of me, and I have no right to hold anything back.

COMMITMENT OR SURRENDER

I always thought the word commit showed such maturity,
And as I gave my life to Christ, I thought this was the key.
But then I heard a story about a foreign land
Where Christians didn't just commit but left
all in God's hands.

They seemed to truly understand why Jesus came to die,
And in their poverty and pain, on Him they would rely.
You see, the word surrender is what God really asks,
He wants to know that I am His, a decision that will last.

Commitment still gives me the choice, to follow as I please.

Surrender gives all choice to Him,
and I just bow my knees.
So now my heart is lighter, my cares have eased away,
To Christ I've given everything, and it's a brand-new day!
-Carol Hopson

COME AND DINE...

1. Are you having a difficult time surrendering all you are and have to the Lord? If yes, write out what you are fearful of.

2. Define what you think it means to be a Christian without giving all to Jesus. Is that possible? What does that kind of thinking produce?

3. Read Hebrews 13:15 and write down in your own

words what we need to do to surrender in difficult times.

4. Feast on 2 Timothy 2 and write out the following:

Instructions:

Promises:

What stood out to you the most that you will apply to your life right now?

There are only two kinds of people in the end: those who say to God, "Thy will be done," and those to whom God says, in the end, "Thy will be done."
-C. S. Lewis

BREAKFAST #5

Preparing the meal...

GOD'S POWER IN MY WEAKNESS

And He said to me, "My grace is sufficient for you, for power is perfected in weakness." Most gladly, therefore, I will rather boast about my weaknesses, that the power of Christ may dwell in me. Therefore I am well content with weaknesses, with insults, with distresses, with persecutions, with difficulties, for Christ's sake; for when I am weak, then I am strong."

-2 Corinthians 12:9-10

Are you boasting about your weaknesses today? How about rejoicing over insults and difficulties you are facing? Well, I haven't done it very often either, but God is teaching me new things about my weaknesses and struggles. I'm learning that they are a very important part of learning humility and strength...my humility and God's strength!

While preparing to speak to a group of young people, I felt extremely weak and inadequate, and as I approached the day of the message, I felt even worse. I was having a bad hair day, bad clothes day, and even my shoes weren't right. Here I was, a grandma, going to speak to bright, intelligent, very with-it Christian university students, and I looked like their grandmother-and I felt even older. What could I say that would interest them? How could I keep their attention and know what they needed to hear? It was at this point, about an hour before my message, that God brought the above passage of Scripture to my mind. In the past, I always seemed to focus on "*My grace is sufficient for you...*," which was great, and I loved it. But I didn't usually dwell on the part about being "*content with weaknesses*" because that was how God would be glorified in my life.

God so lovingly brought to my mind that I was having a problem with pride. I wanted these kids to think I was a "cool" grandma and that I could inspire them and hold their attention by my words. God rebuked me and said, "*Apart from Me, you can do nothing*" (John 15:5).

As I humbly bowed my head in prayer, I gave up my prideful thoughts and said, "I'm yours, Lord. Use me as You choose today. I'm going to rejoice in my weakness that Your power may be seen in me." I left with a renewed, refreshed, ready heart for whatever God had in store.

As I started my message, I decided to be very transparent with those kids. I told them I was having a bad hair day, bad wardrobe day and even my shoes weren't cute...which any woman knows ruins the whole outfit. But I told them that I was there only to speak in the power of God, to be His waitress. I told them that when you go to a restaurant, the important thing isn't the server or waitress; he or she is just there to serve the meal. The chef is the important one, the one who prepares the meal so that you can get nourishment from it and enjoy it. So I asked that they not focus on the waitress but on the meal that the Master Chef had prepared for them.

When God says His power is perfected in our weakness, I'm here to tell you that you can't hold back His power when you are a willing, weak, surrendered waitress. God's meal for those young people was accepted with so much enthusiasm, and their response to His message was overwhelming. It led to life changes and recommitments, and I am still in contact with a few of them, counseling them in their life issues. This is only because the Master Chef's power was allowed to flow through the weakness of His waitress.

Here are some important things to remember about recognizing our weaknesses:

- By recognizing our weaknesses, we rely on God's amazing grace and power alone to enable us to do His work.

- By recognizing our weaknesses, we give others the grace to fail or not be "perfect."

- By recognizing our weaknesses, we live humbly rather than with pride.

- By recognizing our weaknesses, God gets all the glory!

This is why Paul could say he would gladly boast about his weaknesses! Can you do the same today?

FATHER, WILL YOU CARRY ME?

Father, will You carry me?
I'm tired and can't go on.
I've tried to keep on going, but
I've lost my joy and song.

You see, I tried to do it all
So You'd be proud of me.
But all I did was burn right out
As others 'round me see.

"O precious child, my heart is filled
With joy because you asked
For Me to carry you today
That is my rightful task!

"I've longed to hold you in My arms
And give you peace and rest.
But first, you had to see your need
And willingly confess.

"So now I'm thrilled beyond compare,
These times are far too few,
For now you've given up your pride
And let Me carry you."

-Carol Hopson

COME AND DINE...

1. Identify two or three things that you feel are the weaknesses that continue to make you feel insecure or inadequate.

2. Are you willing to give them over to God and let Him use them for His glory? Write out a prayer of surrender right now.

3. Read 2 Corinthians 12:7-10, and then write down how Paul came to the point of boasting about his weaknesses. Why did he choose to do that?

4. Feast on Galatians 6 and answer the following:

What commands are given?

What warnings are given?

What promises are given?

True humility is total acceptance of the place appointed by God, whether it is in the front or in the rear.

BREAKFAST #6

Preparing the meal...

ARE YOU TAKING GOD'S COUNSEL?

Thy word is a lamp unto my feet, and a light unto my path.
-Psalm 119:105, KJV

Thy testimonies are wonderful; therefore my soul observes them. The unfolding of Thy words gives light....Establish my footsteps in Thy word.
-Psalm 119:129-130, 133

A woman came to me for counsel, and she was miserable...more than miserable...she was bitter, angry, and resentful. I can assure you that it wasn't a pretty sight. Things had not gone the way she had planned in her marriage, and she had to give up her dreams and plans. As I listened and asked questions, I found out that she had a good Christian husband who was just trying to provide for his family, but this required moves and unexpected changes. They had to downsize their home, take fewer vacations, and shop in less exclusive stores for a time, and she did not like it.

As I was sitting there listening, I kept thinking, "What's wrong with this woman? Can't she see that her husband is trying his best and she is making it so much harder for him by her bitterness and resentment? Doesn't she know she is disobeying the Lord?" Good questions! But then I realized that I have had times when I disagreed with God's plans for me and couldn't see that He was doing what was best for me. We often quote Romans 8:28 in situations like this: "*And we know that God causes all things to work together for good to those who love God, to those who are called according to His purpose.*" But we often stop there and don't read on..."*For whom He foreknew, He also predestined to become conformed to the image of His Son...*" (Romans 8:29).

Do you see the "Aha!" moment? It's all about being "conformed to His image" and not about getting our own way! I had the joy of explaining this truth to this unhappy woman. God wanted her to grow in His image, "*make the most of this opportunity*" (Ephesians 5:15-17), and be an encouragement and support to her husband and a shining example to her children. God wanted to teach her to submit out of love for Him, and she was battling it all the way. When the Holy Spirit convicted her of her sin, she was saddened at how far Satan had taken her down the road of bitterness and ugliness. She confessed her self-centeredness to the Lord, and together we prayed for a renewed strength and a desire to go with God's plan for her life. Several weeks later, I received a beautiful note from her husband, telling me of the change in his wife and the difference it made in their whole family.

It's easy to recognize these sinful, selfish attitudes in others, but it's not always so easy to recognize in ourselves...especially when we think we're right! I was sitting in church after listening to some very loud worship music and was trying to prepare my heart for the message. But all I could think was, "Why can't they play quieter songs, ones that I know, maybe even an old familiar hymn or two? This loud music couldn't possibly honor the Lord because I don't like it and it doesn't prepare me to worship." Do I hear any "Amens!" out there? Well, God had quite the lesson for me that morning. The pastor was speaking on Philippians 2:3-4, "*Do nothing from selfishness or empty conceit, but with humility of mind let each of you regard one another as more important than himself; do not merely look out for your own personal interests, but also for the interests of others.*" He went on to say that this meant we were to "prefer one another." In other words, wouldn't it be wonderful if we could be happy that the worship music would minister to the young people of the church and not think of our needs first? And if we were a young person, wouldn't it please the Lord if we desired music that ministered to the more mature people in the church? In such instances, we would prefer that others' needs be met before our own.

I was SO convicted of my self-centered sin that morning! Why did I think that the twenty to thirty minutes of worship music on Sunday morning had to be exactly what I wanted? Why could I not rejoice in the fact that it was ministering to many others? Because I selfishly wanted my way...period! I confessed my sin to the Lord that morning, and God has done a miraculous work in my heart. I asked Him to make this a permanent attitude when the music wasn't my preference, which is most of the time, and He has answered my prayer. He always takes my focus to preferring others in obedience to Him, and now I'm free to truly worship my Lord again. Praise God for the miracles He performs when we confess and then do what His Word says.

To Have My Way

Sometimes I think it would be great
To always get my way,
To have things go as I had planned
And never feel dismay.

But that is foolishness to God
Who knows what's best for me,
For He knows what is needed and
He does it lovingly.

It doesn't feel like love when He
Allows such hurtful things.
But I must know Him well enough
And not keep pulling strings.

And so, as I grow more in love
My own desires grow dim.
I learn to trust my Father's plan
And leave all things to Him.

-Carol Hopson

COME AND DINE...

1. Can you think of areas in your life where you are using God's Word to guide your thoughts and actions on a daily basis?

2. Is there a situation where things are not going well and you haven't even considered going to God's Word for wisdom and guidance? Look up Psalm 32:8; write out what God has promised and what you are missing.

3. Spend some time in prayer, making sure that you truly desire to go through whatever it takes to be "*conformed to God's image*." Read Philippians 2:3-8, and write out what following after God requires.

4. Feast on Psalm 42 and write down what God has spoken to you about in this wonderful psalm.

Other books are written for our information. God's Word was written for our transformation!

BREAKFAST #7

Preparing the meal...

THERE'S FREEDOM IN ME!

You shall know the truth, and the truth shall make you free.

-John 8:32

The world tends to think that Christians live in bondage. But we really live in the truth, and that is total freedom. In John 18:37, Jesus told why He came to earth when Pilate had asked Him, "*What have You done?*" Jesus answers, "You say correctly that I am a king. For this I have been born, and for this I have come into the world, to bear witness to the truth."

All truth is found in God and in His Word, and it is so freeing and life-giving. I don't have to worry about new philosophies, deceitful words of men, the power of evil, what's happening in politics or in our nation...I know the truth about my past, present, and future, and that puts my heart at peace. It doesn't mean I don't pray for others or our leaders or seek to be God's ambassador wherever I go. It does mean that I don't live as a slave to worry, fear, and confusion because I don't know the truth.

Let me give you just a simple, everyday illustration of what it means to know the truth. Just this morning I got up early and decided to go to Starbucks and do some work there for an hour. The change of scenery is good sometimes, as my office is in my home. It also gets me out into the world where I desire to be God's sweet aroma to those around me, and God has truly given me a "Starbucks ministry." I prayed as I drove there that God would use me and open a door of witness. As I ordered my drink, I was talking with the manager and inviting her to church; I had already invited her to the "*Practicing His Presence*" series I had taught, and she seemed interested but couldn't come. As I was walking away, this young lady stopped me and asked if I taught a series on self-awareness (she had overheard the "presence" part of my conversation). I told her that what I taught was about practicing God's presence and told her briefly what that meant to me and how it affected my life.

I was excited...how quickly God had answered my prayer to witness! But she was not interested in my God; she belonged to the Self-Realization Center and said they talked about a different God that she felt comfortable with. I smiled at her and tried to ask her a few questions that would open the conversation further. "What or who is this God, and what do you do with him?" I asked.

She replied, "Well, we contemplate him or her, do yoga and meditate..."

"But who is he, and what is he like?" I asked again.

44

"He's whatever you want him to be. He's good thoughts...good karma."

"So you're telling me that you are really God because you can make him whatever you want in your mind." She didn't agree with that but couldn't come up with a good answer.

I took this opportunity and began to tell her about my God who sent Jesus to die on the cross for me, but she shut me up and said, "Your God isn't comfortable for me. I hate Him. Mine makes me feel good. I don't have to do anything I don't want...just be quiet and meditate!" With that she headed out the door. I told her to have a good day and smiled my biggest smile as she walked away.

What a failure...that didn't go well at all...I really didn't get through to her...what happened? Here's where the truth of God's Word was so freeing for me that day. *"But thanks be to God, who always leads us in His triumph in Christ, and manifests through us the sweet aroma of the knowledge of Him in every place"* (2 Corinthians 2:14). So, what happened? Exactly what God knew would happen! I prayed, I was available, she heard about Jesus, and His sweet aroma of salvation was offered. God knew it, and that was all I was responsible for. Praise God! The darkness that had made me feel like a failure was lifted by the truth of God's Word. You see, the triumph was in my obedience, not the results! That was so freeing to me!

What's important to God is our obedience and availability, not our own ability to do great things! That keeps me focused on loving Him and obeying His Word and leaving all the outcomes of life in His all-powerful hands!

Trusting God in Troubled Times

COME AND DINE...

1. Are you feeling like a failure in a certain area right now? If so, have you been obedient to God's Word in handling that situation? If not, ask for forgiveness right now and begin your day with a clean heart. Write out Psalm 51:10-12 as your prayer.

2. Ask God to help you act on the truths of His Word and then leave the results with Him.

3. Read 2 Corinthians 3:4-5 and 4:7 and write down how this is all possible.

4. Feast on 2 Peter 1:1-10 and answer the following:

How much power do you have for everything you face?

Look up each of the following in a dictionary or concordance and write out what they mean:

   Diligence

Moral excellence

Knowledge

Self-control

Perseverance

Godliness

Brotherly kindness

Love

What promise do we have if we practice these qualities? (Notice that it doesn't say we have to be perfect, only truly desire to practice these things.)

The very best proof of your love for the Lord is obedience...Nothing more, nothing less, nothing else.

BREAKFAST #8

Preparing the meal...

GOD DESERVES ALL WE ARE AND HAVE!

For God so loved the world, that He gave His only begotten Son, that whoever believes in Him should not perish, but have eternal life.
-John 3:16

I count all things to be loss in view of the surpassing value of knowing Christ Jesus my Lord, for whom I have suffered the loss of all things, and count them but rubbish in order that I may gain Christ.
-Philippians 3:8

One of the things I have always loved about my dad is that I have always felt so safe in his care. As a child, I would follow him anywhere he lead me because I knew of his unfailing, self-sacrificing love for me. He was the pastor of a large church, and I remember a time when he asked me to walk to the front of our church in the middle of a Sunday morning service because he wanted to use me as an illustration. There were about a thousand people in our church at that time, and I was only about four years old, but I got right up out of the pew and walked to the front because my daddy had called me and I loved and trusted him.

You probably want to know how he was going to use me, don't you? You see, we always had a huge missionary barrel in the entry of our church, and people were supposed to bring nice clothes, blankets, shoes, etc. to send to the missionaries. We would fill several barrels and then send them off to the missionaries we supported. One day, after seeing that people had donated their "very used underwear" and some "used teabags" for the missionaries, my dad got an idea. He wanted his "flock" to see what we should be giving to God and to His work, and he was extremely saddened at what people were giving. So he had put a huge missionary barrel up on the platform that morning; no one knew why it was there. Then he called me up to the front. As I walked up those big steps, he picked me up and hugged me. With tears in his eyes, my daddy set me down in that big missionary barrel and said, "This is what we should be willing to give to God!" I will never forget it, and neither will the people who witnessed it.

Several years ago, while speaking at a retreat in the Pacific Northwest, I was approached by an elderly woman. She told me her name, which was vaguely familiar but I didn't know why. She asked if she could share something with me, and of course I sat down to hear her story. She told me that she had come to know the Lord in my dad's church over fifty years ago and was just rejoicing in what God had done in her life over the years. Then she said, "Do you remember when you were just a wee thing, and your daddy called you up to the front and put you in that big missionary barrel?" I responded that of course I did. She went on to explain what a turning point that was for her. She had been holding on to her children as her possessions and never thought she needed to release them to God to do with as He chose. She had always feared that God might take them far away. That very night, she surrendered her children to the Lord, and peace flooded her soul. Now, she said, all of her children were faithfully serving the Lord in various parts of the world, and her joy was abundantly above all she could ever ask or think! *"I have no greater joy than this, to hear of my children walking in the truth"* (3 John 4).

What do we give to God on a daily basis? A few minutes of prayer and maybe a little time for Bible study...sometimes we think of Him in our day...but do we give Him our very best, what we love the most? God wants our total devotion and the things we love the most...our children, our treasured desires, our surrendered will, our money, and our complete trust. That day in church made such an impact on me, that my daddy would think that giving me to the Lord was the greatest gift He could give. He didn't ask God to not take me faraway to serve in a foreign country. He didn't ask God to make my life comfortable and remove all obstacles. He asked that God would use me for His glory, however He chose!

God's Word so clearly tells us that this should be our attitude in everything.

> *If then you have been raised up with Christ, keep seeking the things above, where Christ is, seated at the right hand of God. Set your mind on the things above, not on the things that are on earth.*
> -Colossians 3:1-2

> *Or do you not know that your body is a temple of the Holy Spirit who is in you, whom you have from God, and that you are not your own? For you have*

been bought with a price: therefore glorify God in your body.

-1 Corinthians 6:19-20

MAX LUCADO WRITES:

On one side stands the crowd.
Jeering.
Baiting.
Demanding.

On the other stands a peasant.
Swollen lips.
Lumpy eye.
Lofty promise.

One promises acceptance,
the other a cross.
One offers flesh and flash,
the other offers faith.

The crowd challenges, "Follow us and fit in."
Jesus promises, "Follow me and stand out."
They promise to please.
God promises to save.

A basin of water?
Or the blood of the Savior?
God looks at you and asks...
Which will be your choice?

(From A Gentle Thunder)

COME AND DINE...

1. Do your attitudes and daily choices show that you have set your mind on pleasing God with your children, your time, your plans, and your possessions?

2. What is the most difficult thing or person for you to totally surrender to the Lord? Can you explain why that is and what you are fearful of? Does your answer show that you have given all to your Savior?

3. Read Isaiah 41:10, 13 and write out how believing this verse can help you with your fears. Then ask God to help you believe it and claim it.

4. Feast on Philippians 4 and then write down the following:

God's instructions

God's promises

Nothing can get between God and me if...
I live close enough to Him!

Breakfast #9

Preparing the meal...

Getting to Know Your Shepherd

You do not believe because you are not of My sheep. My sheep hear My voice, and I know them, and they follow Me; and I give eternal life to them, and they shall never perish; and no one shall snatch them out of My hand.

-John 10:26-28

When my youngest granddaughter, Lucy, came for a visit at seven months of age, she turned away from my husband and started to cry when he reached for her. And yet, she came willingly into my arms as her mother gave her over to me. What had happened? Why was she afraid of her beloved Papa? We realized then that she hadn't seen him in a long time and therefore didn't remember him. I had recently visited her in their home, so she remembered me. My dear husband was so heartbroken at her response, and it reminded me of how our precious Savior must feel when we don't recognize Him because we've been away for too long.

Let's get reacquainted with our Shepherd by looking closely at what He tells us through the Twenty-third Psalm. I've picked this up from various places, with some parts received in an e-mail, and it has blessed me immensely.

The Lord is my Shepherd...that's a relationship!

I shall not want...that's supplying my needs!

He maketh me lie down in green pastures...that's giving me rest!

He leadeth me beside still waters...that's providing refreshment!

He restoreth my soul...that's the healing I need!

He leadeth me in the paths of righteousness...that's Godly guidance!

For His name's sake...that's my purpose!

Yea, though I walk through the valley of the shadow of death...that's testing times!

I will fear no evil...that's His protection!

For Thou art with me...that's His faithfulness!

Thy rod and Thy staff they comfort me...that's discipline and comfort!

Thou preparest a table before me in the presence of mine enemies...that's hope!

Thou anointest my head with oil...that's consecration!

My cup runneth over...that's abundance!

*Surely goodness and mercy shall follow me all the days of my life...*that's His blessing!

*And I will dwell in the house of the Lord...*that's future security!

*Forever...*that's for eternity!

Don't you just want to stand up and shout hallelujah at this point? I do! But what does God want from His sheep? He wants us to listen to Him, to spend time meditating on His words, praying to Him, and seeking His counsel. Four times in Scripture we are commanded to *"hear His voice"* and not *"harden our hearts"* (Psalm 95:7-8; Hebrews 3:7-8, 15; 4:7).

Years ago, I read that the United States government didn't use fake money to teach Treasury agents to detect counterfeit bills. They only showed them real money over and over until they had every detail memorized. Then, when they saw a counterfeit, it looked so different to them that they were able to instantly recognize it. We spend too much time focusing on the counterfeits in this world and not enough time focusing on the "real thing"! If we focus on God's Word and, by doing so, listen to His voice over and over, we will be able to recognize the "counterfeit" voices much easier. Personally, the counterfeit voices tell me that I need to worry about my future, about the U.S. economy, and what I hear in the news every day. They also say that I need to be overly concerned about my physical appearance and standing up for my rights.

Listening to my Shepherd's voice changes everything! His desire is that I would find my security and hope in Him alone. He wants me to love Him above all else...for who He is...for all He's done...for all He continues to do each day as He leads, guides, and cares for me. You see, getting back to little Lucy, as she began spending time with her Papa, feeling his love, care, and protection, she began to respond with open arms and great affection. She had gotten to know her Papa again! Getting reacquainted with your heavenly Papa will give you peace, comfort, and security in these uncertain days!

MY SHEPHERD'S LOVE

I've read so often the Twenty-third Psalm
And know that it's meant to make my heart calm.
But sometimes I feel like I'm out there alone
With no one to turn to and no one to phone.

So what does this chapter in God's Book relay?
Just how does it help me get through every day?
It tells me that Jesus is my Shepherd dear,
And He will provide and remove all my fears.

He'll nourish and feed me and tenderly care
For all of my longings and times of despair.
But I must stay close and hear only His voice,
Then obeying Him will become my first choice.

-Carol Hopson

COME AND DINE...

1. Do you need to spend more time getting to know your heavenly "Papa"? What might you need to do about that?

2. Read the Twenty-third Psalm from this lesson again, and write out four or five things that you are most grateful for about your Shepherd's care.

3. Think of ways you can be more familiar with your Shepherd's voice on a daily basis and write them down. Proverbs 3:5-6 would be helpful in your answer.

4. Feast on John 10. Write out all you learn about our Shepherd in this passage, and then write a prayer of thanksgiving.

> *He loves not Christ at all who does not love*
> *Christ above all!*

BREAKFAST #10

Preparing the meal...

WHAT VOICES ARE YOU LISTENING TO?

There is a way which seems right to a man, but its end is the way of death.
-Proverbs 14:12; see also Proverbs 16:25

This is one of the few times when God repeats a verse twice...with exactly the same words! Do you suppose it's because we are sheep who are not so smart and need to hear it twice? I think so! Oh, how often we think "our way" is the best way, and we fight against the way God is taking us or leading us.

All the ways of a man are clean in his own sight, but the LORD weighs the motives. Commit your works to the LORD, and your plans will be established.
-Proverbs 16:2-3

As I stood outside the airport in another state, in the rain, and waited for an unknown person to pick me up for yet another retreat, I was discouraged...and even a little angry. I had waited almost three hours so far, and no one had come to pick me up. Of course, my cell phone was dead, and I couldn't locate any number to call anyway, so there I stood...cold, wet, and disgruntled with God's way! You may be thinking that this surely wasn't God's plan, and yet, I had given myself and my day to the Lord to do with as He chose. So, it had to be His way...but I didn't like it! How could these people be so rude and thoughtless! Self-pity had really set in, and I felt like a martyr standing there...suffering for Jesus. But it was all wasted because my heart attitude was not one that pleased the Lord.

When I finally made contact with someone, after borrowing a phone and calling my husband for the retreat leader's number, I was told that they were already at the retreat conference center, which was three hours away. The only problem was that they had forgotten to pick up the speaker! Now I had to wait another hour while someone from the church came and got me and drove me the three hours to the retreat. I arrived after having no lunch, no dinner, and no apology when I arrived. They seemed to think it was quite funny that no one was assigned to pick me up. So, what does this have to do with "my way" versus "God's way"? Let me tell you.

My way was to be angry, very angry, at their lack of sensitivity and planning. My way was to feel very sorry for myself and decide to never come back to this church again, if asked. My way was to just get through the retreat with my focus on getting out of there and getting home! But was that God's way? *"Be ye kind one to another, tenderhearted, forgiving one another..."* (Ephesians 4:32, KJV) came to mind. Would my wounded ego forgive these people? Then I remembered, *"Do all in the name of the Lord Jesus..."* (Colossians 3:17). That meant that even in this situation, my priority was to represent Jesus, to act as He would. The battle raged in me while the worship music played on. You see, I had yet another war going on inside as the fifteen-minute praise and worship part of the service went on for forty minutes. It was now 9:00 p.m. and I hadn't even been introduced yet. I had a one-hour message, which they had notes for, and we were already an hour behind schedule.

Are you getting a feeling for what was going on inside of my very human heart? "*My sheep hear My voice and they know Me and they follow Me...*" "OK, Lord, I am Your sheep, a very weary, frustrated sheep, but I will follow and leave all my anger and frustration in Your hands." At that moment, God began healing me and gave me a renewed desire to serve Him at any cost. The battle came and went over and over during the weekend, but each time I had to say, "I'll follow Jesus!" The last morning of the retreat, we had more than fifty decisions for Christ...both new believers and recommitments. Praise God for His work in all of us...especially me! Do you want to know the rest of the story? They invited me back the next year...and I went! And yes, I was picked up immediately this time!

God's way was to do a work in me...to teach me that life and ministry are not about me! He was reminding me that I'm not in this for comfort or to receive special attention, but I'm doing this work because He called me to it...for His glory, not mine! As I put my injured pride aside, God drew me closer to Himself, and I could again thank Him for another lesson in humility and trust.

COME AND DINE...

1. Have you been offended or slighted by someone recently? Is it still bothering you? Be honest.

2. Do you want to follow your Shepherd and obey His words and walk in His way? If you do, write out what you will do about it. Read 2 Corinthians 4:7-18 and Ephesians 4:29-32.

3. Read Proverbs 15:1-7 and write out what God says about our speech.

4. Feast on 1 Peter 2; write out what God speaks to you about in this great chapter. Did you learn something new? Were you convicted about anything?

Sometimes the Lord calms the storm. Sometimes He lets the storm rage and calms His child.

Breakfast #11

Preparing the meal...

Beware of Distractions

Brethren, I do not regard myself as having laid hold of it yet; but one thing I do: forgetting what lies behind and reaching forward to what lies ahead, I press on toward the goal for the prize of the upward call of God in Christ Jesus.

-Philippians 3:13-14

Distractions are like Krispy Krème doughnuts! They're so enticing and seem so harmless when you're indulging. As I sat in Starbucks this morning, I observed a mother feeding her five- or six-year-old child Krispy Krème doughnuts and hot chocolate for breakfast. Now believe me, it looked delicious to me, and the child was certainly enjoying all of it. But I began to think about what that breakfast would produce later, and I began to pity the teacher who would have this child in her classroom. After being in education for over forty years, my husband and I have seen the consequences of all that sugar in a little body, and it isn't good at all. What that precious child needs is a good, healthy, nourishing breakfast that helps the brain function properly and gives the body the vitamins and proteins it needs to grow strong.

As I left that morning, I thought of all the distractions that can cloud our lives...distractions that are so satisfying for the moment, but the lasting effects are detrimental to our physical or spiritual health and keep us from the important things God has planned for us. What are some of those distractions?

- The desire for financial gain leading to fear, anxiety, or overwork

- The desire to cheat, just a little bit, to get ahead

- The desire to lower my convictions to gain popularity

- The desire for recognition or the need to feel important

- The desire for an easier life, to always get my way

- The desire to fill the void in our lives with eating, shopping, busyness, etc.

- The desire to have more things-bigger home, better car

- The desire to be so busy that we don't have to face God's truths

Where do all these distractions come from, and why are they so enticing?

Let no one say when he is tempted, 'I am being tempted by God'; for God cannot be tempted by evil,

*and He Himself does not tempt anyone. But each
one is tempted when he is carried away and enticed
by his own lust.*

-James 1:13-14

It is our own lusts, which are part of our old nature, that draw us into temptation. That's why Paul said "this one thing I do." He was always focused on moving forward in love and obedience to the Lord. Then when distractions came, he knew it wasn't part of "the one thing" God had called him to do. You see, Philippians 3:14 says that Paul was always pressing toward "the goal" or "the mark." This was a picture of someone running a race and always focusing on the goal line, or the picture of someone shooting an arrow at a target in archery; they always had to keep their eye on "the mark" or the target, because that was their whole purpose-to hit the mark.

My dear parents are now ninety-three and ninety-five years of age. They have spent their lives serving the Lord in various churches and mission organizations. By God's grace, they still live in their own home, on my brother's property, so they have family right there if needed. Both of my parents have had serious health issues: heart attacks, strokes, perforated colon, multiple cancers. And life is not easy for them. Just getting through each day is hard work, and yet they choose to be together in their own home, with daily helpers who come for a few hours. Last week, while sitting in his chair, my dad had something happen, and he was sure God was taking him home, so he lovingly prepared my mother and told her that he was going to glory. They then called my brother and sister-in-law who came right over and lovingly took charge from there. My dad didn't go to glory that night, and God is again strengthening him for a few more days on this earth, but he and my mother are so ready to be with Jesus! His comment to me on the phone was, "I'm so ready for God to take me home, but if He has some purpose for leaving me here, I'll try to be faithful."

Today I received the following e-mail from my dad:

Dear Carol and Jim,

We have some big news to share with you. Our all night lady, who started with us several days ago when I needed some extra help, came to us a little religious but not saved. She is married to a man who wants nothing to do with God. She had some very keen problems in the past with a broken home, etc., but her grandfather was a preacher. We have been working with her and sharing with her each evening. One evening she said that she knew the Lord brought her to us, but she was not ready to make a decision. I told her we would not push her, but I tried your approach, Carol. I told her that God loved her so much that He wanted her to be in heaven with Him, and we wanted her to be there. I gave her a New Testament and marked some verses for her to read. Each evening she sat and watched a Gaither video with us and seemed to enjoy it, and then we would pray.

Last night was her last night with us, and when we prayed, I asked dear mother if I could pray for her in any way. Then I asked our helper if I could pray for anything for her, and she said, "YES!" I asked her what it was, and she said, "I have made the decision to accept Jesus as my Savior." Praise the Lord! Our living room became a delivery room immediately, and we saw and heard a new "delivery" while she was "born again." I just had to shed a few tears of joy, and I gave her a big hug. She mentioned again and again how she knew that God had brought her to us for these ten days just for this very reason. It was so wonderful!

At age ninety-five, my dad was still focused on "this one thing" that God had called him to do! Don't "miss the mark" because you're focused on all the distractions, or on desiring an easier life, rather than on fulfilling God's purpose for you. Krispy Krème doughnuts can never compete with a new birth into God's family!

Therefore, we are ambassadors for Christ, as though God were entreating through us; we beg you on behalf of Christ, be reconciled to God.
                                                    -2 Corinthians 5:20

COME AND DINE...

1. What things tend to distract you from staying focused on "the goal" God has called you to run toward?

2. Why do you think you are easily led astray by those things? Are they more enticing than walking with the Lord?

3. Read 1 Peter 1:23-2:3, and write down how Peter illustrates the importance of God's Word in our daily lives. (When we are not consistently in God's Word, we forget what's truly important and get sidetracked more easily.)

4. Feast on Romans 8:1-25, and write out all the "meat" God teaches us in this passage.

The Bible contains the vitamins of soul health.

BREAKFAST #12

Preparing the meal...

TOTAL PEACE AVAILABLE!

Peace I leave with you; My peace I give to you; not as the world gives, do I give to you. Let not your heart be troubled, nor let it be fearful.

-John 14:27

For He Himself is our peace...

-Ephesians 2:14

When God called Jesus our *"Prince of Peace"* in Isaiah 9:6, it meant that He would be the ruler or administrator of peace, both now and in the future. It further means that He wants to rule in our emotions, thoughts, and actions and bring peace to our minds at all times. If He is our peace and if He left His peace with us, why don't we have it? Let me suggest three reasons why we might lose our peace.

1. We are focusing on our problems rather than on the power and presence of God in our lives.

When I do this, I'm plagued with sadness, bitterness, anger, or anxiety. I met someone on a flight who was really struggling, so I tried to encourage her and gave her some scriptures to help her. She claimed to be a Christian and was grateful. About six months later, God brought her to mind, and I e-mailed her and asked how she was doing. She answered that she was really going under because of the political situation, finances, and her work. God was so good to allow me to send her what I had just been studying from His Word and how it was continually helping me to stay focused on God's Word rather than on what was going on around me (1 Corinthians 2:5; Psalm 112:6-7; 119:165). She was so thankful to God for seeing her need and sending an e-mail from many states away that would bring her back to the truth and to spiritual health. She wrote, "The verses you sent are now my lifeline to peace! I've stopped focusing on the problems and keep these words always before me."

2. We focus on what we don't have rather than on all we do have.

I once counseled a woman who had a lovely home and lots of "things," but she wasn't satisfied. She always wanted more-a bigger house, fancier car, and more expensive vacations. She was now brokenhearted because her husband had left her for another woman. This new woman was thrilled with the house, car, and lifestyle he provided for her. It was heart-wrenching to see her pain and know that her attitude and response to God's Word could have changed everything and probably would have saved her marriage. God so clearly says, *"Let your character be free from the love of money, being content with what you have, for He Himself has said, 'I will never desert you, nor will I ever forsake you'"* (Hebrews 13:5).

The famous Bible scholar, Matthew Henry, was once attacked and robbed by thieves. That night, he wrote these words in his diary: "Let me be thankful first, because I was never robbed before; second, although they took my money, they did not take my life; third, because although they took my all, it was not very much and fourth, because it was I who was robbed, not I who robbed."

Oh, how I love his attitude and what he chose to focus on. I read this over twenty years ago, and I have truly never forgotten it. In fact, in difficult times, I try to think of four things, like Matthew Henry, that I can be thankful for, and it always brings my heart to praise. I'm choosing to "rejoice by choice!"

3. We focus on people and allow them to rob us of our peace.

I am so guilty of this one! I have let so many people rob me of my peace. Sometimes it was my husband or one of my children. Other times it was a friend or co-worker or someone in ministry that didn't treat my husband or me in a fair way. **But it was always my choice to give up my joy, be angry, and lose my peace**! David learned this so well when he said, "*This I know, that God is for me. In God, whose word I praise, in the LORD, whose word I praise, in God I have put my trust, I shall not be afraid. What can man do to me?*" (Psalm 56:9-11). It's interesting and important to note that he reminds himself in four different ways to put his trust in God...then he concludes with, "I shall not be afraid. What can man do to me?" The key is to put your hope and expectations in God alone!

TO KNOW DAILY PEACE:

1. Quickly recognize when you are focusing on problems or people.

2. Confess it and change your thoughts to ones that honor the Lord.

3. Focus on all you have in Christ, and choose one new thing to praise God for all day long.

4. Choose, with God's help, to focus on pleasing the Lord with your words, thoughts, and actions rather than letting your emotions control you.

Remember that peace comes when our heart comes into agreement with God's heart...not the opposite!

WHAT HAPPENED TO MY PEACE?

What happened to my peace today? I had it yesterday.
Did someone come and steal it and then just run away?

How did I give it up so fast, why did I not hang on?
It seems that oh, so suddenly, I lost my joy and song.

Let's see, what was I thinking, when my peace disappeared?
Oh yes, I now remember, I focused on some fears.

And then I listened to some words that hurt down deep
inside, and suddenly my joy was gone,
oh, what a downward slide!

What must I do to get it back? I so much want to rest
in what my Lord has promised, but I think I failed the test.

Oh yes, that's music to my ears, I know Your Word is true!
You say, "Just turn your heart to Me, for I've forgiven you.

Then focus not on what you hear or think or feel or see.
But on the truths of My own words, for they will set you free."
-Carol Hopson

COME AND DINE...

1. What or who most often robs you of your peace?

2. Write out what your expectations were and what led you to turn away from having a peaceful heart.

3. Read all of Psalm 56, and write what David understood about God and the choices he made to trust God.

4. Feast on Psalm 103, and write down all the ways God showers us with His benefits. (I find it absolutely overwhelming!)

Before we can enjoy the peace of God, we must know the God of peace!

Breakfast #13

Preparing the meal...

Victory in the Trials of Life

Consider it all joy, my brethren, when you encounter various trials, knowing that the testing of your faith produces endurance. And let endurance have its perfect result, that you may be perfect and complete, lacking in nothing.

-James 1:2-4

This is always a difficult passage to read, to believe, and to teach. I have been asked over and over how we can consider it "all joy" when terrible things happen in our lives. I know that I can't understand the mind of God, so at times, it's hard to give adequate answers. However, in looking at the meaning of joy and perfect, it has helped me grasp the meaning of this passage a little more clearly.

First of all, the meaning of joy is "a state of well-being that comes from trusting God completely." **It has nothing to do with our circumstances and everything to do with our relationship with and trust in God**. It seems that trials and adversity are God's tools for spiritual growth. If we aren't interested in maturing in Christ, we'll struggle greatly with our trials and circumstances.

A woman came to me who was furious with her husband for moving her to California and away from her family in another state. She was so miserable and so mad at her husband that she couldn't see beyond her loneliness and anger. She had heard me speak on accepting what God brings into our lives and using it for His glory, but she was unable to see how it applied to her situation. She was totally blinded by her own perspective...wondering how God could use her when she was lonely, miserable, away from her family, and upset with God. I asked her if she had given her life to the Lord, and she responded that she had. "So when did you take it back?" I asked. She was stunned for a moment and then asked what I meant. "Well, when you give something away, it doesn't belong to you anymore; you have no rights over it. So, since you are claiming all the rights over your life, I'm assuming that you took it back and really didn't mean it when you gave it to the Lord."

"But I don't like what He's doing!" she cried to me.

I then went on to ask her if she had given Him a chance to show her what He could do in her, for her, and through her if she let go of her selfishness, confessed her sin, and allowed God to work. I asked her to close her fist and picture me trying to give her a lot of money...would she be able to receive it with a closed fist? No, it would fall to the floor. But if she opened her hand, she could receive the gift I was giving to her. I used this to explain to her that her mind was like that closed fist and she couldn't see or receive any of God's blessings until she opened her mind and heart to receive them. God did open her eyes and revealed to her that this misery she was relishing wasn't any fun, and she finally admitted her sin and repented.

Now it's time to explain the word perfect, because our verse says that when we endure trials, they will have their "perfect result" in us. The word perfect here means that we will mature, we will grow, and we will be more like Christ through each trial. We can rejoice in trials because the end result is our growth! If our priorities are ease, comfort, and self-will, we will see our trials as stumbling blocks rather than stepping-stones to maturity.

This dear wife decided to try to open her eyes and heart to what God might be doing in moving them to this new place. I met with her several times, and after a few months, she could hardly believe that she had been so unhappy. God had provided great friends, a wonderful church family, great weather, new excursions to the beach and elsewhere with her family, and much more. But it wasn't until she was willing to let go of her selfish agenda that she could see what God wanted to give her.

I have to admit that I have had a closed fist at times too, especially when I didn't like the direction God was leading. But as I've opened my heart to do His will, not mine, He has poured out His blessings in ways I never expected. No, things didn't always go as I would choose or plan, but God always brought peace, joy, and a closer walk with Him through it all.

In this you greatly rejoice, even though now for a little while, if necessary, you have been distressed by various trials, that the proof of your faith, being more precious than gold which is perishable, even though tested by fire, may be found to result in praise and glory and honor at the revelation of Jesus Christ.

-1 Peter 1:6-7

PLEASE HELP ME, LORD

Dear Lord, sometimes it's difficult
To follow where You lead.
It seems that my plans differ so
And I know what I need.

But that is selfish arrogance
Since I belong to You.
O help me, Lord, to see things from
Your heavenly point of view.

And help me keep an open mind
For what Your love can do.
And as I trust Your perfect plan
I know You'll see me through.

-Carol Hopson

COME AND DINE...

1. What hinders you from finding joy in your trials?

2. Look at a recent trial or difficult time, and write out how you could have grown in your faith if you had trusted God with it. (If you did "rejoice" in your trial, explain what God brought into your life to mature you.)

3. Read 2 Thessalonians 1:11-12, and write down why we need to be obedient in this area of rejoicing in the difficult times God allows.

4. Feast on James chapter 5, and write out all the promises you find in this chapter; then spend time thanking God for them.

God sends trials not to impair us but to improve us.

BREAKFAST #14

Preparing the meal...

ARE YOU WILLING TO SUFFER FOR ME?

For you have been called for this purpose, since Christ suffered for you, leaving you an example for you to follow in His steps, who committed no sin, nor was any deceit found in His mouth; and while being reviled, He did not revile in return; while suffering, He uttered no threats, but kept entrusting Himself to Him who judges righteously.

-1 Peter 2:21-23

In all of my counseling over the years, this seems to surprise people the most...that God says we have been called to suffer. Many Christians believe that when they become part of God's family, they receive a ticket to a pain-free life, and then they are discouraged, distraught, or even devastated when difficult trials come their way. We don't always know the purpose of our suffering, but God does give us clear direction as to how we are to handle it. We are to "commit no sin" when wronged or when enduring trials, and we are told to "utter no threats" because we can entrust ourselves and our situation to God, who will be the Righteous Judge. For me, it has been incredibly freeing to realize that God will make everything just in His time, so I don't need to be bitter or take my own revenge. Trusting in my trials is entrusting all to Him...my life, my reputation, my character, my future, my pain...and accepting how He decides to handle it.

David was certainly no stranger to suffering. At the end of his reign, David's sons rose up and rebelled against him, causing great pain in his last days. His son Absalom, who was eventually to take the throne, sought out some of his followers and persuaded them to overthrow David. Absalom also sat outside the city gates and pretended to be a very caring leader who would understand people's struggles, and gradually he gained quite a following. Then, David's nephew and favorite counselor turned on him and joined with Absalom and his followers to overthrow him. At this point, David had to leave all of his comforts and beautiful palatial surroundings to flee to the desert when he discovered that Absalom, his own son, had planned to take his life. Can you even fathom this kind of pain and betrayal?

It was when he was hiding out in the desert that he penned Psalm 63. Let's look at the choices David made while in the midst of great suffering.

1. "O God, You are my God; early will I seek You..." (v. 1, NKJV).

First of all he recognizes and reaffirms that "You are my God." He was stating his personal relationship with and commitment to Almighty God no matter what his circumstances were.

Secondly, David knew that he had to begin his day seeking the Lord, focusing on Him and not on how unfair his situation was. That would only bring him down, so he chose to wake up and seek God's direction. He didn't waste time in self-pity and destructive thoughts; he went to the only One who could give him comfort.

2. "My soul thirsts for You; my flesh longs for you in a dry and thirsty land where there is no water" (v. 1, NKJV).

Next, David longs for the comfort of God's presence as you would long for a drink in the dry desert. This truly shows the heart of someone who loves the Lord above all. It is no wonder that God called him a "man after God's own heart." You might think that David would cry out for God to restore his position and undo all the unfair, hurtful situations he was facing. But David knew that above all else, the most important thing in life was to be in God's presence, because that's where true joy was found. "Thou wilt make known to me the path of life; in Thy presence is fullness of joy..." (Psalm 16:11).

3. "So I have looked for You in the sanctuary, to see Your power and Your glory" (v. 2, NKJV).

David is now asking God that he would be able to see Him and worship Him in the desert, without the ark of the covenant, as he did in the tabernacle. He now knew that God's presence wasn't limited to buildings or certain times of formal worship. So he asked to see God's power and glory right where he was. Isn't that what we need to do when we are in a desert?

4. "Because your lovingkindness is better than life, my lips shall praise You. Thus I will bless You while I live" (vv. 3-4, NKJV).

David now realizes that nothing...not kingdoms, palaces, power, earthly security, or anything else...compares to God's loving-kindness, which will never leave him. Oh, how he must have loved God to come to this realization while fleeing to the desert. Because he truly believes it, he says, "My lips shall praise you. Thus I will bless You while I live." He wants to spend his last hours praising the Lord, not fighting for what he thinks is fair. He was willing to leave all in the hands of "Him who judges righteously."

5. "I will lift up my hands in Your name" (v. 4, NKJV).

As an Old Testament posture of prayer, lifted-up hands were a picture of sending prayers up to God, as well as a readiness to receive that which God gave back to the believer. It was an outward evidence of putting one's trust in God alone, and that is what David is doing here. He also must have realized that God would be the Righteous Judge of all the wrong that was done to him, so he didn't have to seek his own revenge. That's what we were reminded of in the opening verse...that Jesus kept "entrusting Himself to Him who judges righteously" (1 Peter 2:23).

Are you facing troubled times right now? Does life seem unfair? I've certainly been there. I have felt that God surely wasn't seeing what was happening to His child. But that is never truth! *Do not fear, for I am with you; do not anxiously look about you, for I am your God. I will strengthen you, surely I will help you, surely I will uphold you with My righteous right hand*" (Isaiah 41:10). God is still in control, and all He allows is for my good and growth. I pray that in today's problems, as well as in future trials, I will be ready to seek Him first, that I will long for His presence to fill my mind and heart, that I will eagerly spend my day praising Him for His loving-kindness, and finally, that I will willingly lift my hands in a prayer of surrender to and acceptance of His will for my life.

THE OTHER SIDE

God is weaving day by day
A pattern full of color,
Full of twists and turns galore,
That doesn't match another.

It may look like a big mistake
When glancing at it here,
With knots and loose ends dangling,
Making patterns quite unclear.

Sometimes hopeless it may seem
Because it doesn't fit
With what you thought 'twas all about
And what your life would knit.

But Sovereign God designs your days
When in Him you abide.
And someday when you see His face,
You'll see the other side.

-Carol Hopson

COME AND DINE...

1. Does your suffering take your eyes off of your Savior, or does it make you focus on Him much more?

2. What should our suffering and trials bring about in our lives? (Read 1 Peter 1:6-8; Psalm 119:67, 71-72.)

3. Look again at the five choices David made while in the emotional and physical desert, and then write them out in your own words and make them applicable to your own situation.

4. Feast on all of Psalm 63 and write out all of the praises and truths David declares.

It's not the greatness of our troubles but the smallness of our faith that makes us fearful.

Breakfast #15

Preparing the meal...

Understanding Your Purpose!

According to my earnest expectation and hope, that I shall not be put to shame in anything, but that with all boldness, Christ shall even now, as always, be exalted [magnified] in my body, whether by life or by death.

-Philippians 1:20

My eyes are getting older, like the rest of me, and it gets more and more difficult to see things clearly. To read anything up close, I now need glasses to magnify the words and make them easy for me to read. Without my glasses, words and sentences are blurred and make no sense. In the above verse, Paul states that his hope and purpose is to "exalt (or magnify)" Christ whether by life or by death. Let's think about what a "magnifier" does. Does it clarify or blur? Does it make things easier to see or more difficult to see? Does it enlarge or minimize things? Of course, the value of the magnifying glass is in how well it clarifies, enlarges, and makes something easier to read. That's its whole purpose.

What is your purpose today? Did you think of all you have to accomplish...the chores... the errands...caring for your family? Those are all good things that do need your care. But the overall purpose in doing all of these things should be to magnify Christ in the way you handle things today. Will your family see that you are making Christ's love, joy, and peace clearer for them to understand by the way you speak and act? Colossians 3:17 reminds us, "*Do all in the name of the Lord Jesus...*," which means to do all as if "representing Jesus" to those around you.

I was not in the best frame of mind one morning. I had company again, and now we needed to take them on a tour of the area, the Christian school where my husband ministered, and so on. We had done this many times with many people, and I had so many other things to do and was a little annoyed that I had to do this again! After complaining to God in my prayer, He got my attention and clearly reminded me, through Philippians 1:20, that my purpose was not to have my way today but to let Him have His way...with a joyful attitude. "*Rejoice in the Lord always; again I will say, rejoice!*" (Philippians 4:4).

With a new attitude, we left the house to show our friends the area, the beach, some of the special sights, and then the Christian school. As we were walking through the campus on a Saturday morning, we ran into a teacher and introduced her to our guests. After walking on, the Holy Spirit prompted me to go back and talk with that dear teacher as I had seen something in her face and heard discouragement in her voice. I excused myself and let my husband continue the tour while I went back to find the teacher. As I approached her, I asked if there was anything

I could do for her as God had sent me back because He loved her so much and cared about her. Could I pray with her about anything?

This precious soul broke into tears and said, "How could you know that I'm so broken inside and the pain is more than I can bear?" As I wrapped my arms around her, she told me the story of a tragedy that had just happened in her family, and she didn't know who to talk to or where to turn for help. God, in His love, had heard her cry and sent me, on a Saturday, when no one is usually at the school, to be His loving arms, ears, and voice. "*I waited patiently for the LORD; and He inclined to me, and heard my cry. He brought me up out of the pit of destruction, out of the miry clay...*" (Psalm 40:1-2). And to think that I had not wanted to do what God had planned for me that day because I had my own plans! I was able to spend time praying with her and helping her to know what to do and how to give her pain to the Lord and leave it for Him to work out. It began a wonderful relationship with this dear child of God.

You see, I was concerned about my agenda and getting "my important things" done. God was concerned about His agenda to meet the deep needs of one of His children...and He wanted to use me. Thank You, God, for the great joy of being Your servant!

CAN YOU USE ME, LORD?

Can I help a friend today,
does someone have a need?
Maybe I could share a word,
a smile, a hug, a deed.

Can You use my hands, dear Lord,
to give a gentle touch?
Sometimes a willing, helping hand
can mean so very much.

Can you use my voice, dear Lord?
Does someone need to hear
That there is One who sees her hurt
and knows her deepest fears?

Can you use my life, dear Lord?
Your servant I will be,
For leading others to the cross
is what means most to me.

-Carol Hopson

COME AND DINE...

1. Can you think of three ways to "magnify" Christ as you go about your day today?

2. Write down what thoughts keeps you from being available for God to use as His light to your family and to those with whom you have contact today.

3. Feast on Philippians 1 and answer the following:

What did Paul believe about his circumstances? (List the verses by your answer.)

What did Paul believe about his purpose? (List the verses.)

What promises do you find in this chapter?

When praying, don't give God instructions...
just report for duty!

BREAKFAST #16

Preparing the meal...

DO YOU NEED WISDOM?

His name will be called Wonderful Counselor, Mighty God, Eternal Father, Prince of Peace.

-Isaiah 9:6

If I were to introduce my husband to you, I could say, "This is my husband, Jim, and I love him." That tells you just a little bit about Jim...that he's married to me and that I love him. But suppose I told you that my husband was a very special man, a committed Christian, a wonderful father to his children, an incredible grandfather, a passionate Christian school administrator, a devoted and loving husband, a faithful friend, a respected mentor...now you would really know who my husband was. You heard lots more names, and it revealed so much more about his character. So it is with God. As I've been studying God's character, I've seen how His names reveal so much about Him, and I fall in love with Him more and more.

Do you find the counsel you get in the world confusing at times? I do! You hear that you are to do this or that when raising your children, and then the next year you're not supposed to do it...it will damage them. You hear that we should always stand up for our rights, we're number one, don't give in to anyone, and yet the Bible says we are to humble ourselves...and on it goes. That is why I'm so thankful that God has revealed Himself as our "Wonderful Counselor." This means that He is an exceptional or distinguished Counselor. His words are unique, and they will meet our emotional and spiritual needs. David knew this when he wrote, *"Thy testimonies also are my delight; they are my counselors"* (Psalm 119:24).

While I was speaking at a retreat recently, I was suddenly verbally attacked for the scriptural truth I was teaching from Ephesians 5:22-23, where we are told, *"Wives, be subject to your own husbands, as to the Lord."* In the middle of the meeting, a woman stood up and tried to shame me for my teaching. She remained angry with me until the very end of the retreat, though I tried to speak with her several times. What should I do in this situation? Tell her how rude she was? Demand an apology? Put her in her place? Ignore her? Argue my point? If I relied on my emotions at this point, I would be in big trouble, so I knew that wasn't the answer. And so, because God is my Counselor through His Word, I remembered that I was to speak the truth in love and give grace to the hearer (Ephesians 4:16, 29; Colossians 4:6). That meant that I was to respond in love and give unmerited favor to the one who had disrupted the meeting and attacked me. So, only by the grace of God, I smiled at her and said, "I know that this can be confusing for some, and it's difficult to understand the first time you hear it, but I'm sharing what God says works the best for our marriage relationship. He's the One who made us and designed the institution of marriage. The Bible is His manual for how we are to live and how we can find peace, purpose, and fulfillment in the life He designed for us. I'd be happy to talk further with you after the meeting if you'd like, and I do understand your concern." With that, I smiled again and moved on. You could hear a huge sigh of relief in the audience as I moved to the next part of the message. How thankful I was for Colossians 4:6, which also counseled me, "Let your speech always be with grace, seasoned, as it were, with salt, so that you may know how you should respond to each person."

Without God as my Counselor, I would have been angry and disturbed; I would have lost track of my thoughts and who knows what else. I also might have tried to avoid her all weekend, as she really was angry and caused quite a disturbance in the meeting. However, by the very end of the retreat, she came to me at the book table and told me how much she learned and how much she loved being at the retreat…she even bought a couple of books…then she gave me a hug and was gone. Praise God for His counsel!

I need God's divine counsel every day of my life, or else my emotions seem to take control. I especially need Colossians 3:12-13, which says, "*And so, as those who have been chosen of God, holy and beloved, put on a heart of compassion, kindness, humility, gentleness and patience; bearing with one another and forgiving each other, whoever has a complaint against anyone; just as the lord forgave you, so also should you.*" Can you even imagine how our families, our neighbors, our workplace, and the world would be impacted if we as Christians just obeyed the counsel in these two verses?

COME AND DINE...

1. Do you think first of what God would counsel you to say or do in any situation? If not, why not? Do you need to memorize some of the above verses so the Holy Spirit can bring them to your mind when needed?

2. Write down how going to God's Word for counsel would spare you from anger, stress, and unneeded conflict. (See Colossians 3:12-17.)

3. Read the familiar passage in Galatians 5:22-25 and see what the "fruit of the Spirit" looks like in our daily lives. Do you see that it doesn't say "fruits," as if they are separate and we can pick and choose which ones we want to obey? How can you apply these to your life today? (Try to be specific in your answer.)

4. Feast on Psalm 37 today, and then write out the counsel you receive from this passage. (You should find at least ten things in the first eleven verses.)

At the close of a meeting, a cynic approached Mr. Moody and said, "Mr. Moody, during your address this evening, I counted eighteen mistakes in your English." Looking at his critic, Mr. Moody kindly answered, "Young man, I am using for the glory of God, all the grammar that I know. Are you doing the same?"

BREAKFAST #17

Preparing the meal...

CHANGING YOUR PERSPECTIVE

Joseph said to them, "Do not be afraid, for am I in God's place? And as for you, you meant evil against me, but God meant it for good in order to bring about this present result, to preserve many people alive."

-Genesis 50:19-20

Have you ever found yourself saying or thinking any of the following statements?

- If only this situation wouldn't have happened...

- If only I could do my life over...

- If only I wouldn't have been betrayed by someone I loved...

- If only I would have made a different choice in my mate or my job...

- If only I had more money...

- If only my kids would have turned out differently...

- If only I didn't have these physical problems...

- If only I wouldn't have made that mistake...

- If only I could be someone different...

Many Christians have a lot of "if onlys" in their lives, and these keep them from all God wants to do in them, for them, and through them. I have found that when I say "if only," I need to go to God for a new perspective, one that honors Him. Why not turn your "if onlys" into "what ifs"?

Here are three new ways to think about your situation.

1. What if God is allowing this situation for my growth, to make me more like Him?

2. What if I'm missing great opportunities God has planned for me because of my bad attitude or wrong thinking?

3. What if I could use each circumstance in my life to please the Lord?

Joseph was betrayed by those he loved, forgotten by those he trusted, lied to, horribly mistreated, falsely accused...and yet God allowed all of it so that he could be used for God's purpose...to bring about the result God intended. Paul saw prison as God's place for him, and Daniel saw the lions' den as God's place. Each situation was a terrifying, unfair, undeserved situation, but God was faithful, powerful, and had a bigger plan. The key was that Joseph, Daniel, and Paul all trusted God to use their circumstances, no matter how unfair they were, for God's glory.

When my husband and I started a Christian school, we had little or no money. We had bills to pay and teachers' salaries due, and we had no money for any of it. We had followed God's clear leading to start the school, and we had faith that He would see us through, but we didn't have enough students in those early months to pay the bills. Now, we were faced with payday and didn't have near enough money to pay our staff and teachers...let alone ourselves. For a few minutes those "if onlys" invaded my mind. If only we hadn't left secure jobs in a great Christian school, if only we had a big donor who would have provided the funds for this year, if only we had more students, and so on. I also wondered why God hadn't provided the needed finances since we had stepped out in faith and obedience to Him to start this school. Why would He put us through such hard times where it looked like He wasn't providing...where we'd have to tell the teachers that there was no money to pay them?

Since I was the secretary and bookkeeper, I walked into my husband's office and told him the problem. We decided to spend some time praying for God's wisdom and direction. Maybe we should try to take out a loan or call someone to help...but who? Then we knew we would simply call on the Lord and see how He would lead. With a peaceful heart, I walked back into my office to find a woman standing there waiting for me. I thought maybe she was interested in enrolling her children in the school, so I asked her if she'd like information about the school. Here is what she said: "I've never done anything like this before, but there was a detour through town that brought me right by your school. When I saw your school sign out front, I had this extremely strong sense that I was to stop my car and come in here and write you a check. I don't live here and have never been through here before, but I think God wants me to give you this." She handed me a check and was gone as quickly as she appeared. I was in shock and ran to the door to thank her as she headed back to her car. When I got back to my office, I looked at the check, and it was just what we needed for that month!

Can you even imagine the rejoicing, the chapel time of praise with our students, and the faith-building that came because of that one event? Humanly, it looked like an "if only"…but with God it was a "what if" moment. "What if I want to show you My loving provision in a miraculous way? What if I want to teach you to walk by faith and not by sight? What if I want to give you a new testimony that will enable you to trust Me through twenty-five more years of ministry?" That's exactly what He did!

In Philippians 1:6 Paul says, "*For I am confident of this very thing, that He who began a good work in you will perfect it until the day of Christ Jesus.*" Paul could accept all of his circumstances, good or bad, fair or unfair, wanted or unwanted, because he was "confident" that God was at work and would continue to use him until He returned.

COME AND DINE...

1. What are some of your "if onlys" that you cling to right now?

2. God does want to mature you through how you handle the disappointments and detours of life. What steps will you take to look at your "if onlys" with a new perspective?

3. How will Psalm 46:1-3, 10-11 help you?

4. Feast on Philippians 1, and write out how Paul chose to use his circumstances to bring glory to God. Write out his attitudes and actions and the accompanying verses.

God's sovereignty and love aren't measured by the difficulties He helps us avoid or the pleasant circumstances He allows us to enjoy, but by His ability to accomplish His purposes through every circumstance.

Breakfast #18

Preparing the meal...

You're Offered a Clean Heart!

Create in me a clean heart, O God, and renew a steadfast spirit within me....Restore to me the joy of Thy salvation, and sustain me with a willing spirit.
-Psalm 51:10, 12

Have you tried to clean up your own heart? I have, and it doesn't work. When I was deeply hurt by someone's words and actions, I tried over and over to free my heart from anger and resentment. However, it would only work for a short time, and then the old emotions would take over again. I tried thinking happy thoughts, and I tried ignoring the problem altogether, but neither proved successful. I was definitely losing control of my heart. Have you struggled with the same thing lately?

Even today, your heart might hold resentment, jealousy, or an unforgiving spirit. Do you wonder why it's so difficult to get rid of those feelings? Let's look to God's Word and see what David prayed in Psalm 51. First of all, he says, "*Wash me thoroughly from my iniquity, and cleanse me from my sin. For I know my transgressions, and my sin is ever before me. Against Thee, Thee only, I have sinned, and done what is evil in Thy sight...*" (vv. 2-4). You see, David realized that his sin was against God and that he needed to repent, turn away from that sin, and seek God's forgiveness. So, he needed to desire a heart change first of all and then repent of his thoughts and actions.

Secondly, he realized that he had no power to cleanse his own heart, so He asked God to create a clean heart in him. The word create here denotes "to make from nothing," so David realized that there was nothing good in himself; it was all rotten, and only God could give him a clean heart. And thirdly, he knew that he would only be sustained or kept free from sin by having a "willing heart" to do God's will (v. 12).

Let me illustrate this with a story. My husband and I had gone away for a ten-day camping and fishing trip to Mammoth Lakes. We had looked forward to it so much and had a great time relaxing, fishing, enjoying the family, and exploring the great outdoors. However, after ten days, it was a good feeling to pull into our driveway and get back to our own beds, but we had loved the time together. As we opened the garage door, we noticed a strong odor...what could it be? We walked toward our extra refrigerator-freezer that we kept in the garage and could hardly stand the smell. My husband bravely opened the door, and we about passed out! You see, the electricity had gone out while we were gone, and the temperature soared. So we had a freezer full of rotten salmon that my husband had caught on a previous fishing trip. You can't even imagine the stench.

I'm pinching my nose as I write this just thinking about it.

Well, what should we do? We closed the door quickly, got out Clorox and Pine-Sol and all our cleaning supplies, and scrubbed the outside of that freezer until it was spotless...wow, it looked like new! But the smell was still there and getting more pungent. Why was that? Because we hadn't emptied the cause of the stench, the rotten contents!

There have been times in my life when I've tried to scrub the outside of me to make me look good to others, but the sin was still inside-and it wasn't pretty. There is absolutely no victory without emptying the rotten contents of sin. What might some of those rotten contents look like?

- I just can't forgive this person!

- I want to nurse this injustice a little longer and get even.

- My life is so unfair, and I'm so angry about my circumstances.

- I just can't tolerate people who have a different, "sinful" point of view.

- I'm so angry. I don't know why this has happened; I deserve better.

- I don't like my marriage and I want out, no matter what God says.

- I think my plan is better than God's plan, so I'm going to try mine.

All of these say that God has made a mistake or He isn't

powerful enough to help me forgive or honor Him in my circumstances. These are sinful choices and must be confessed before we can have a clean heart that is ready for God to use. "*No one can serve two masters; for either he will hate the one and love the other, or he will hold to one and despise the other. You cannot serve God and mammon [man]*" (Matthew 6:24). In order to trust God in troubled times, we must be willing to empty the rotten contents of our self-centered life and accept the "new life" God offers us.

In his book A Gentle Thunder, Max Lucado writes:

Here is (dare I say it?) the greatest miracle of God. It is astounding when God heals the body. It is extraordinary when God hears the prayer. It is incredible when God provides the new job, the new car, the new child. But none of these compares to when God creates new life.

At our new birth God remakes our souls and gives us what we need, again. New eyes so we can see by faith. A new mind so we can have the mind of Christ. New strength so we won't grow tired. A new vision so we won't lose heart. A new voice for praise and new hands for service. And most of all, a new heart. A heart that has been cleansed by Christ.

And, oh, how we need it. We have soiled what he gave us the first time. We have used our eyes to see impurity, our hands to give pain, our feet to walk the wrong path, our minds to think evil thoughts. All of us need to be made new again.

"CREATE IN ME A CLEAN HEART, O GOD..."

A CLEAN HEART

Create in me a clean heart, God,
And keep me steadfast too.
I want to be your servant, Lord,
Please show me what to do.

"My precious child, it's in My Book
So keep that in your mind.
If you will read it, then obey
My will you'll surely find.

"A willing heart is what I ask,
And faith to trust My plan.
For this will keep your heart from sin
When you don't understand."

-Carol Hopson

COME AND DINE...

1. Has God revealed some ugly contents that you haven't dumped yet? Confess them to God right now and find the joy of a clean heart. (Write down what He has shown you so you don't forget. :)

2. Read Matthew 7:24-27 about the parable of the two foundations. Which one are you building on when you choose sin over God's way? Write out what the "rain and winds and floods" might refer to in your life right now.

3. Feast on Matthew 6:19-34 and answer the following:

What treasures can you lay up in heaven right now?

What warnings do you see in these verses?

What commands are given?

What do you learn about God's care for you?

The most expensive thing in the world...is sin!

BREAKFAST #19

Preparing the meal...

MEETING THE PERFECT FATHER

If you then, being evil, know how to give good gifts to your children, how much more will your Father who is in heaven give what is good to those who ask Him!

-Matthew 7:11

His name will be called Wonderful Counselor, Mighty God, Eternal [Everlasting] Father...

-Isaiah 9:6

Here is another name that reveals who God is and how He desires to relate to us as our Everlasting Father. This is the relational aspect of His character. It means that He is forever doing what is good for us out of His great love for us as His children.

Do you have a great, loving relationship with your earthly father? Many that I talk with do not, and it is very difficult for them to love and accept God as their Father, especially if they have an abusive or unloving father. I often tell these dear people to make a list of all the things that would describe the "perfect father," and then we see how God matches up with their list. Here is a new way to look at the character of God and how He desires to relate to you.

1. He loves me unconditionally.

For I am persuaded, that neither death, nor life, nor angels, nor principalities, nor powers, nor things present, nor things to come, nor height, nor depth, nor any other creature, shall be able to separate us from the <u>love</u> of God, which is in Christ Jesus our Lord.
-Romans 8:38-39, KJV, emphasis added

2. He thinks I'm special and beautiful.

For we are His workmanship [beautiful poem], created in Christ Jesus for good works, which God prepared beforehand, that we should walk in them.
-Ephesians 2:10

I will give thanks to Thee, for I am fearfully and wonderfully made; wonderful are Thy works, and my soul knows it very well. My frame was not hidden from Thee, when I was made in secret, and skillfully wrought in the depths of the earth.
-Psalm 139:14-15

3. He wants to protect Me.

You are my hiding place; You shall preserve me from trouble; You shall surround me with songs of deliverance.
-Psalm 32:7, NKJV

The righteous cry out, and the LORD hears, and delivers them out of all their troubles. The LORD is near to those who have a broken heart, and saves such as have a contrite spirit.

-Psalm 34:17-18, NKJV

4. He would sacrifice His life for me.

The Father knows Me and I know the Father; and I lay down My life for the sheep.

-John 10:15

For God so loved the world, that He gave His only begotten Son, that whoever believes in Him should not perish, but have eternal life.

-John 3:16

5. He cares about all my concerns.

If I say, "My foot slips," Your mercy, O LORD, will hold me up. In the multitude of my anxieties within me, Your comforts delight my soul.

-Psalm 94:18-19, NKJV

He brought me up out of the pit of destruction, out of the miry clay; and He set my feet upon a rock making my footsteps firm.

-Psalm 40:2

6. He forgives me every time I fail or hurt Him.

If we confess our sins, He is faithful and just to forgive us our sins and to cleanse us from all unrighteousness.

-1 John 1:9, NKJV

7. He responds to my weakness with love.

"My grace is sufficient for you, for power is perfected in weakness." Most gladly, therefore, I will rather

boast about my weaknesses, that the power of Christ may dwell in me.

-2 Corinthians 12:9

8. He will always be there for me.

Let your character be free from the love of money, being content with what you have; for He Himself has said, "I will never desert you, nor will I ever forsake you."

-Hebrews 13:5

9. He corrects me out of love.

Whom the Lord loves He reproves, even as a father, the son in whom he delights.

-Proverbs 3:12

For those whom the Lord loves He disciplines.

-Hebrews 12:6

He [God] disciplines us for our good, that we may share His holiness.

-Hebrews 12:10

10. He will give me guidance in life's decisions.

I will instruct you and teach you in the way which you should go; I will counsel you with My eye upon you.

-Psalm 32:8

The steps of a man are established by the LORD; and He delights in his way. When he falls, he shall not be hurled headlong; because the LORD is the One who holds his hand.

-Psalm 37:23-24

11. He will train me for everything I need in life.

All Scripture is inspired by God and profitable for teaching, for reproof, for correction, for training in righteousness; that the man of God may be adequate, equipped for every good work.

-2 Timothy 3:16-17

But the Helper, the Holy Spirit, whom the Father will send in My name, He will teach you all things, and bring to your remembrance all that I said to you.

-John 14:26

12. He will be a perfect example.

Have this attitude in yourselves which was in Christ Jesus, who, although He existed in the form of God, did not regard equality with God a thing to be grasped, but emptied Himself, taking the form of a bond-servant, and being made in the likeness of men. And being found in appearance as a man, He humbled Himself by becoming obedient to the point of death, even death on a cross.

-Philippians 2:5-8

13. He would make plans for my future.

He who believes in Me shall live even if he dies, and everyone who lives and believes in Me shall never die….Let not your heart be troubled…I go and prepare a place for you…

-John 11:25-26; 14:1, 3

14. He holds my hand in fearful times.

When he falls, he shall not be hurled headlong; because the LORD is the One who holds his hand.

-Psalm 37:24

Do not fear, for I am with you; do not anxiously look about you, for I am your God. I will strengthen you, surely I will help you, surely I will uphold you with My righteous right hand.

-Isaiah 41:10

If you're still feeling afraid or unloved, it's because you don't really know your heavenly Father. As you spend time with Him through prayer, reading His Word, and worshipping with other believers, you will begin to see how much He loves you, and you will stop living by Satan's lies and will begin living in truth. That is when you will learn the great joy of trusting Him with all you are and have.

COME AND DINE...

1. Which aspects of your heavenly Father's love do you need to feel and claim the most right now?

2. Write out how believing these truths will change your life, your self-image, and your walk with the Lord.

3. As you've read about your heavenly Father, can you write out a prayer that puts your trust in Him...no matter what your fears are?

4. Feast on John 1:1-18, and then write out the facts you find about Jesus and God. Be sure to write out how you become a child of God the Father. (Also read Romans 10:9-10 for your answer.)

He who is born of God should grow to
resemble His Father!

Breakfast #20

Preparing the meal...

Trust God for the Impossible!

His name shall be called Wonderful Counselor, Mighty God...

-Isaiah 9:6

Who is the King of glory? The LORD strong and mighty, the LORD mighty in battle.

-Psalm 24:8

I love to know that I have Almighty God caring for me, protecting me, and handling all the impossible situations in my life! The problem is that I don't always remember this or keep Him in His proper place in the battles of life. This name for God was given to show that He was mighty and strong in battle. When you have God as your all-powerful leader, do you wait until the last minute and all else has failed to call on Him? Of course not! You put Him at the front of the battle lines to defeat the enemy. El Gibbor is the One who wants to be our protection in the daily battles. He wants to go before us and defeat the enemy, but we often forget and only call on Him when we are at the end of our rope.

For fifteen years of our ministry in Christian schools, we provided all-school skate nights at a local skating rink once a month. They were great fun, with lots of spills and thrills, but I learned a lot about human nature there. My husband and I would always be on hand to help the young first-timers stay on their feet and learn to skate. Most of them loved the attention and learned quickly after a few trips around the rink with one of us. (I can still feel the sore arms I'd wake up with the next morning!) But there were always those who refused help and wanted to do it on their own. As we watched them struggle, fall, cry, and finally give up, we'd again remember how much wisdom there is in accepting help from someone older, stronger, and wiser. It's just that way with our mighty God! To experience His power and victory in battle, we must remember to always surrender ourselves and our situation into His care.

God says we are all like sheep that are constantly straying (Isaiah 53:6), and when sheep choose to stray, they are no longer under their shepherd's protection. They have chosen to run from it and be on their own. In the same way, we make the same mistake when we think we can handle our problems better than God can or when we just forget He is there and don't call on Him. God won't work things out for us if we're taking control of our own lives...and fighting against biblical principles.

I've counseled many in marriage situations where one or the other decides to have an affair, do their own thing, justify it, abandon their family, and then wonder why they don't have peace or feel God's presence anymore. They even tell me that they know God wanted this for them because they weren't happy in their marriage. Oh, how shameful this is...to think that you can walk away from all of God's principles and still expect His protection.

This illustration seems so clear to us, doesn't it? And yet we do the same thing when we decide to worry about our children, our health, our finances, or politics and walk away from the peace that God offers if we would only trust Him. Then we wonder why we're miserable and can't feel God's presence with us. Guess who moved?

While getting more and more frustrated over the political situation and the direction our nation was heading, I was convicted about getting all worked up over something that God has clearly spoken to me about in the past. So I had to confess my worried and angry heart and go back to God's Word for direction and peace. It was then that God gave me two verses that calmed my heart completely: "...*your faith should not rest on the wisdom of men, but on the power of God*" (1 Corinthians 2:5). "*He [the righteous] will not fear evil tidings; his heart is steadfast, trusting in the LORD*" (Psalms 112:7). I truly can't even put into words the peace and trust God gave me that day as I left all my worries and frustrations with Him. He then led me to sit down and write out twenty ways I could honor Him in these uncertain, unstable times. (I've included these in the appendix at the end of the book.) This list has gone out all over the world via the Internet. As I began sharing it with others who were struggling, they would ask for it and would then share it at church or with their Bible study group or send it to relatives in other states and countries. Our mighty God (El Gibbor) was at work and transformed my thinking, and then used what He taught me to encourage and strengthen others. He is always willing and able to take on the battles for us, but we must let Him.

You need not fight in this battle; station yourselves, stand and see the salvation of the LORD on your behalf....Do not fear or be dismayed; tomorrow go out to face them, for the LORD is with you.

-(2 Chronicles 20:17

Do You Need a Miracle?

Do you need a miracle
For what you face today?
Are you stressed and fearful?
Do you want to run away?

Does life seem overwhelming?
Has hope grown, oh, so dim?
Does it seem impossible
To find true peace within?

Then you are at a good place
For God to work His plan.
So put all thoughts in His care
And remove it from your hands!

He wants so much to help you
And give you peace within,
But you must give up your plan
And leave all things with Him.

-Carol Hopson

COME AND DINE...

1. What would be different in your life if you put El Gibbor up front on the battle lines every day?

2. What might you do to help you remember to set your thoughts totally on His power and might in something that you are worried about today?

3. Read Psalm 58:9-10, 16-17, and then write out why David could sing and praise God while being pursued by his enemies.

4. Feast on the nourishment in Psalm 40, and then write out five things you can put into practice today as you put El Gibbor on the front lines of your battles.

> *Our strength is shown in the things we stand for. Our weakness is shown in the things we fall for.*
> -Hugh Cowan

Breakfast #21

Preparing the meal...

Where to Go in a Storm!

Those who love Thy law have great peace, and nothing causes them to stumble.

-Psalm 119:165

I will never forget Thy precepts, for by them Thou hast revived me. I am Thine, save me; for I have sought Thy precepts.

-Psalm 119:93-94

"I've trusted God with my problems, and He just keeps letting me down! He doesn't answer my prayers, and nothing is working out as it should!" Have you ever felt this way? Many Christians have...they look around at their families, their health, their finances, their future, their country, and feel like God isn't answering their prayers. Could it be that God is answering our prayers, but we just don't like the answers because we don't understand what He is doing?

The book of Philippians is written by the apostle Paul from a prison cell. Do you think that is where he expected to be when he set out on a missionary journey to serve God...to encourage believers...to be a light in darkest Rome? Probably not! But Paul knew some very important truths, and he based his life on those principles in every storm of life.

Let me explain by telling you about some dear friends of ours. They live in "tornado territory" in the Midwest and are often faced with great weather dangers. When I asked how they lived with that, they said, "We all have to listen for the storm warnings (sirens) that warn us of danger, and we heed them immediately and get ourselves to safety. If you heed the warning, you will be just fine." They went on to assure me that shelter and protection were available for them; they just needed to know where to go, and then they must go without delay.

For some reason, this reminded me of the storms in my own life. I've been hit with a few tornados in my years of ministry, and sometimes I've heeded the warning sirens, but other times I've let the storm do great damage because I wasn't going to the "storm shelter" of God's Word for protection. Let's get back to Paul and see how he could write "the book of joy" while being chained in prison.

As I look at the fourth chapter of Philippians, I see the warnings that he heeded...no matter what his circumstances were.

1. **He knew he needed to keep rejoicing!** "*Rejoice in the Lord always; again I will say, rejoice!*" (v. 4). Paul wasn't rejoicing in his circumstances, the tornadoes, or seemingly unanswered prayers; he was rejoicing in his

Lord. He knew that God would see him through anything He allowed, and he chose to rejoice that God was using him for His purposes. He wasn't focusing on himself but on the "big picture" of God's plan for his life.

2. He knew not to worry about his circumstances!
"Be anxious for nothing, but in everything by prayer and supplication with thanksgiving, let your requests be made known to God. And the peace of God, which surpasses all comprehension, shall guard your hearts and your minds in Christ Jesus" (vv. 6-7). Paul realized that belonging to God meant that he could take every burden or fear to Him and leave it for Him to take care of. He focused on obedience and left the end results for God to work out. This, then, brought total peace in any situation…even while chained in prison.

3. He knew he had to guard his thought life!
"Finally, brethren, whatever is true, whatever is honorable, whatever is right, whatever is pure, whatever is lovely, whatever is of good repute…let your mind dwell on these things" (v. 8). It would have been so tempting to think on how and why he had been beaten and put into prison. It would have been normal to focus on those who persecuted and arrested him, but he knew that would lead to discouragement and disobedience.

4. He chose to be content with whatever God allowed! *"Not that I speak from want; for I have learned to be content in whatever circumstances I am"* (v. 11). Why could he be content in all circumstances? Because he had given his life to the Lord to do with as He chose, and he trusted God completely. Remember that he wrote, *"For to me, to live is Christ…"*

(Philippians 1:21). He didn't say, "*For to me, to live is Paul.*" Therefore, he was content.

5. **He knew where his strength came from!** "*I can do all things through Him who strengthens me*" (Philippians 4:13). Paul knew not to try to handle life's "tornados" and struggles in his own strength, so he called on God's strength for everything he faced. He realized that nothing was impossible with Almighty God and that whatever He allowed, He would see him through.

Are you heeding the warnings God has given? Think of a ship at night, with its lights blinking. The captain sees another light in the distance, and he also realizes a collision is inevitable. He sends out an emergency message that says:

> "Emergency! Collision inevitable! Change your course ten degrees to the South!"

> The answer comes back from the light in the distance, "Emergency! Collision inevitable! Change your course ten degrees to the north!"

> The captain of the first ship gets a bit frustrated and says, "I am the captain!"

> To which the light in the distance replies, "Emergency! Collision inevitable! Change your course ten degrees to the north. I am a third class seaman!"

> The captain of the first ship is now furious. He sends out his previous message and adds, "I am a battleship!"

And the answer comes back from the light in the distance, "Emergency! Collision inevitable! Change your course ten degrees to the north! I am a lighthouse!"

God's Word is the "lighthouse" that keeps us safe from the destruction of the tornadoes in these troubling times. *"Thy Word is a lamp to my feet and a light to my path"* (Psalm 119:105). Are you heeding the warnings and running to safety?

COME AND DINE...

1. Read again the five "tornado warnings" that Paul focused on. Write down which one stands out to you right now.

2. Think of a present circumstance or storm in your life, and write down how this warning or direction would keep you from suffering the consequences of wrong choices. (Use more than one if you choose.)

3. Look up the following verses and write what they say about the importance of "light":

Psalm 27:1

Isaiah 2:5

Matthew 5:14

Ephesians 5:8

1 John 1:7

4. Feast on Psalm 119:65-104, and then write what the benefits of being in God's Word are and what our attitude toward His Word should be.

The world crowns success, but God crowns faithfulness.

Breakfast #22

Preparing the meal...

What Are You Afraid Of?

Why are you in despair, O my soul? And why have you become disturbed within me? Hope in God, for I shall yet praise Him, the help of my countenance, and my God.

-Psalm 42:11

In the past month, I've asked many people what they are most afraid of. Here are some of the answers I've received:

- I'm afraid that I won't have enough money for retirement.

- I'm afraid that I'm going to be laid off soon.

- I'm afraid that I might get cancer.

- I'm afraid that my children might make destructive choices.

- I'm afraid of suffering with a painful illness for a long time.

- I'm afraid of the direction our country is heading.

- I'm afraid that God might take one of my children away from me.

- I'm afraid that God might ask too much of me.

- I'm afraid that my situation will never get better.

These are all fears that many people struggle with at some point in their lives. Because of the unknown, we prime the pump of worry and then spiral down into fear and end up very stressed or even depressed. But does God's Word ever tell us to be stressed, worried, or fearful? I haven't found that in God's Word, and I've been studying it for more than forty years, so why are we fearful?

I think we get afraid when we think we won't like what God might allow and we fear that it will be too difficult to handle. Years ago, my husband was leaving for a three-week mission trip to a third world country, and I wasn't able to go due to the cost. We were excited about this privilege for him and the ministry he was going to have. I anticipated it all with him and helped him plan and pack and then took him to the airport. (Keep in mind that this was when we had no e-mail and no cell phones to stay in contact, so I knew that I might not hear from him for the whole three weeks.) As I bravely said good-bye, I thought I was doing pretty well considering we had been married for over thirty years and had never been apart for more than a few days.

However, on the way home, the tears began to blur my eyes, and they just kept coming. I began to think, "What if I never see him again on this earth? What if that was the last time he hugs me or the last time I hear his sweet voice?" That was all it took for the flood that followed. I had to pull off of the freeway and find a place to park so that I could pour out my heart to God. Let me tell you that I was very surprised by this, because I had always thought that I trusted God with my family and really hadn't lived in fear. But I was suddenly overwhelmed with the possibility of losing my husband.

As I sat beside the freeway and cried, I asked God to show me where this fear came from and what I should do about it. He so clearly showed me that my fear came from an unwillingness to accept "whatever" God chose for me! You see, if I was willing for God to take my husband home to heaven whenever He chose, there would be nothing to fear. So my fear came from thinking I might not be able to handle life without him. After God revealed that to me, the next step was very clear…I had to give Jim up to the Lord to do with as He chose. I had to tell God that should He decide that I would never see my husband again on this earth, that I would still trust Him, love Him, and serve Him. I didn't know all of the answers, but I knew God would take care of me. His word promises just that!

This I recall to mind, therefore I have hope, the LORD'S lovingkindnesses indeed never cease, for His compassions never fail. They are new every morning; great is Thy faithfulness.

-Lamentations 3:21-23

As I let go of the worst that could happen and trusted God with it, He removed all my fear and replaced it with His peace. "*I sought the LORD, and He answered me, and delivered me from all my fears*" (Psalm 34:4). Satan had nothing left to work with, so my heart was truly at peace. And it stayed that way during the whole three weeks he was gone.

If you're living in fear, stop and ask yourself the following:

- What is the worst thing that can happen?

- Do I believe that God will still be in control if that happens?

Even from eternity I am He; and there is none who can deliver out of My hand; I act and who can reverse it?
                                                    -Isaiah 43:13

My purpose will be established, and I will accomplish all my good pleasure.
                                                    -Isaiah 46:10

The LORD will accomplish what concerns me; Thy lovingkindness, O LORD, is everlasting.
                                                    -Psalm 138:8

- Do I believe that God can and will give me peace no matter what?

Do not tremble, and do not be afraid; have I not long since announced it to you and declared it? And you are my witnesses. Is there any God besides Me, or is there any other Rock? I know of none.
                                                    -Isaiah 44:8

Do not fear, for I am with you; do not anxiously look about you, for I am your God.
                                                    -Isaiah 41:10

Peace I leave with you; My peace I give to you...
                                                    -John 14:27

- Do I believe that this world is not my home and the best is yet to come?

Let not your heart be troubled; believe in God, believe also in Me....I go to prepare a place for you. And if I go and prepare a place for you, I will come again, and receive you to Myself; that where I am, there you may be also.

-John 14:1-3

COME AND DINE...

1. What are you most afraid of? Write it out and look at it.

2. Are you willing to put this into God's hands, knowing that He loves you and gave His life for you?

3. Do you believe that God created you to glorify Him in all situations? Look at the following verses for your answer and write what they say:

1 Peter 2:9

Philippians 1:20

Matthew 5:16

1 Corinthians 6:20

Colossians 1:10

2 Timothy 2:4

4. Feast on Isaiah 40, and then write out three or four truths that will help you the most when you are tempted to be fearful.

I would fear for my life, had I not already given it away.

BREAKFAST #23

Preparing the meal...

DO YOU WANT TO KNOW GOD'S WILL?

If anyone wishes to come after Me, let him deny himself, and take up his cross daily, and follow me.
                                                            -Luke 9:23

It seems that one of the most common things I hear from women when speaking or counseling is, "If only I knew what God wanted me to do!" Some have even said, "I wish He'd just write me a letter and tell me!" I always reply, "Guess what; He did write you that letter." And then I take them to this verse in Luke 9:23. Often it's not what they want to hear, but let me share how it helps us to know God's will in any situation.

First of all, to know God's will we must **deny self!** Yikes! That's definitely not popular to say these days! This means that we need to renounce self as the center of our life and actions and realize that life is not about me but about how I can reveal and reflect God to those around me. In my book *The Journey From Feelings to Faith*, I've included a personal checkup to see if you're living for self or for God. So, when difficulties, trials, or changed plans come...

If living for self (denying God):

● You'll ask, "Why is this happening to me? It's so unfair."

● You'll despair that "This isn't what I want and I don't like it."

● You'll decide that "I guess God's plan doesn't work for me."

● You'll lose hope and become angry, bitter, and discontent.

If living for God (denying self):

● You'll say, "It's not my choice, but I'll trust God with it."

● You'll decide, "I need to see what verses might help me through this."

● You'll ask, "I wonder how I can grow to be more like Christ through this?"

● You'll then pray, "Dear God, please use this situation for Your glory!"

Can you see the difference it makes when we are willing to say no to self and yes to God...no matter what? "*I delight to do Your will, O my God*" (Psalm 40:8, NKJV).

The second thing we see in Luke 9:23 is that we are to "***take up our cross daily***." This does not mean that we are to carry our burdens; it means that we are to accept our circumstances as part of God's plan for us and then seek to glorify Him in how we handle them. To take up our cross daily is to take what life brings, and God allows, and seek to use it for God's glory. *"Let your light so shine before men, that they may see your good works and glorify your Father in heaven"* (Matthew 5:16, NKJV).

Notice that there are no escape clauses here, such as...

- Let your light shine except when you're suffering...

- Let your light shine except when you've been unfairly treated...

- Let your light shine unless you don't really understand what I'm doing...

- Let your light shine...when you feel really good about life!

What are those good works that others will see? Sometimes it's the fruit of being faithful when suffering, of being patient when wronged, of being loving when feeling unloved, of being forgiving when you've been mistreated.

I remember a time when a very dear friend had hurt me deeply, and I didn't understand why. She had turned on me for seemingly no reason and had pulled away without even a phone call. Now, I cherish my friends and work hard at being a good friend and being there for them, especially in the hard times. So this was really hard for me to accept, and it became an emotional cross that I was bearing daily because it left such a void in my life. After suffering for weeks, I went to God's Word and He brought me to the passage in John 13:1-

5 where Jesus is about to wash the disciples' feet. I was struck first by the words in verse 1: "*He loved them to the end.*" Even knowing of Judas' betrayal, He still loved him. And then as an act of humility and obedience to His Father, He took a towel and washed the disciples' feet.

Tearfully I read and reread this portion of God's Word. Was I willing to "take a towel" and humble myself and go to my friend and seek to restore the friendship, even if I wasn't at fault? After praying over this, I gave her a call, and she agreed to meet with me. Let me just tell you that I was a little anxious and not at all sure how I could get through this. But I needed to do what God's Word had convicted me to do, and so I went in and met with her. All of my worries and fears fled when I saw her tear-stained face, and I reached out to embrace her. The healing had already begun by the simple act of "taking up my cross" and seeking to honor the Lord with my attitude and actions.

Thirdly, Luke 9:23 declares that God's will is for us to "***follow Him.***" So, what does it mean to follow Him? John 10:27 gives us the answer: "*My sheep hear My voice, and I know them, and they follow Me.*" Following God means that we are to listen to His voice, and only His voice, and then go where He leads.

Here are some important things to know about listening to God's voice:

1. You must bring God into every aspect of your life.

   This happens through prayerful fellowship throughout the day, studying and meditating on God's Word, and truly desiring to do His will in all situations.

2. You must be ready and willing to obey God's Word in every area of life.

This means surrendering your life and will to God so that whatever His Word tells you becomes your heart's desire.

3. You can't be practicing sin and expect to hear God's voice.

When you are practicing sin (doubting, worrying, being bitter, having an unforgiving heart, etc.), you have broken your fellowship with the Lord, and so you can't hear His voice.

4. You must give up what you think God should do and accept what He says to do.

When you are holding on to something that you really want, such as not wanting to move or leave your comfort zone or have to forgive someone, you can't truly be open to what God is trying to show you because your personal preference is affecting your perspective. **To know God's will you must surrender your will!**

Deuteronomy 30:15, 19-20 sums this up beautifully: "*See, I have set before you today life and prosperity, and death and adversity....So choose life in order that you may live...by loving the LORD your God, by obeying His voice, and by holding fast to Him.*" The voices you listen to each day will truly determine your behavior and actions. Will you worry and wither, or will you trust and triumph? Will you choose to bring light or darkness to those around you?

I'M YOURS, LORD

I just can't think of how I'd want
To live my life today
If I were just living for me
With nothing in my way.

I can't just think of how my rights
Are stepped on every day,
And how I'd like to tell someone
Their plan is in my way.

I can't just do what humanly
Seems right to those around
Or spend my time on fruitless goals,
So many can be found.

I can't react to what I hear
With anger or with pride
Or dwell on thoughts that hurt my soul
And dwell down deep inside.

Why can't I choose to do these things?
Why have a different view?
"Because I love You, Jesus, and
My heart belongs to You!"

-Carol Hopson

COME AND DINE...

1. Which part of the three commands in Luke 9:23 is the most difficult for you to obey? Why?

2. Reread the important things about listening to God's voice, and write down where you might need to change your thinking, actions, or daily patterns.

3. Feast on Romans 6, then answer the following questions:

What does it say about our "old self" or old nature?

What does it teach about being "dead to sin" and "alive to God"? How would that apply to the instructions in Luke 9:23?

How are we to look at sin now that we are "dead to sin"?

What incredible victories are promised?

Adversity removes the cloak of "what we are supposed to be" to reveal the truth of what we are.
-Charles Stanley

Conclusion

O for Grace to Trust Him More!

As I come to the end of this book, I am again amazed at how God works so miraculously to accomplish His purpose. I was positively certain that my writing season was over after the eighth book, and I was SO relieved! You see, it is truly not my desire to write books, and each one has been accomplished only by God's grace. However, when God decides He wants me to start writing, He absolutely overwhelms me with the need to be obedient and get typing...and it then becomes my "love gift" to Him. By God's grace and power alone, I can hardly type fast enough as He pours Himself into every word. At times, my dear husband has to come and tell me to stop and take a break, because the direction and leading from God are so strong.

Humanly, I always feel that I have nothing of importance to say, but God seems to want to use my weaknesses and my experiences to help others learn to trust Him in their troubled times. And so I willingly trust Him to see me through and then ask Him to use it all for His glory alone. My part is obedience...period!

What do you think God's purpose is for you? Are you looking toward a certain goal that you want to accomplish? *In My Utmost for His Highest*, Oswald Chambers writes:

> What is my vision of God's purpose for me? Whatever it may be, His purpose is for me to depend on Him and on His power now. If I can stay calm, faithful, and unconfused while in the middle of the turmoil of life, the goal of the purpose of God is being accomplished in me. God is not working toward a particular finish-His purpose is the process itself....**It is the process, not the outcome, that is glorifying to God**.

No matter what God has allowed in your life right now, no matter what heartaches or difficulties you are experiencing, God is calling you to be faithful to Him in the process. I pray that this book has helped you understand how to do just that. Sometimes the struggles are huge...and other times it's something as simple as aging.

Growing older happens to every human being, and no one can escape it, yet it isn't always easy to deal with or accept. But even in the process of aging, it is my desire to trust God with each new wrinkle and age spot I see, because even this can be used for God's glory.

ON AGE SPOTS AND WRINKLES

There's age spots and sun spots and wrinkles galore
And each day I wake up, I see a few more.
What happened to that youthful face I once knew?
Who is this old person that comes into view?

O Lord, help me see what's important to You.
I know You don't want me to worry and stew
About things that naturally come on with age,
So help me accept and enjoy this new stage.

And help me to focus on doing my best
To represent You in this world full of stress.
And then I won't care about what others see,
The age spots and wrinkles won't matter to me.

For aging is part of Your wonderful plan
As You take me through life with Your loving hand.
And then when my purpose on earth is complete,
I'll get a new body...oh, won't that be neat!
                                        -Carol Hopson

And then there are the larger issues, like all we see happening in the world around us. It can truly be overwhelming and very discouraging at times, and yet God tells us, *"Trust in the LORD with all your heart; do not depend on your own understanding"* (Proverbs 3:5, NLT). So God is more interested in what is going on in my heart than what is going on in the world. He wants me to trust Him, obey Him, and find my purpose in serving Him...especially in these "troubled times."

THIS WORLD'S OFF TRACK

What's happened to this world of ours?
It seems all out of whack.
I feel like everything I see
Is truly way off track.

In movies, songs, and MTV,
There is no moral code.
They flaunt their sin, draw others in,
And lead down darkest roads.

What can I do to make a change
In what this world believes?
I'm only one and not so strong,
What can my life achieve?

I'll start by living life each day
To share God's love and grace.
I'll look for opportunities
To someone's fears erase.

And then I'll pray for leaders strong
Who'll hold fast to God's Word.
I'll share the news and use my vote
So my voice will be heard.

Then finally, I'll keep in mind
That God is in control
And He wants me to trust Him more
And pray and lead and grow.

I cannot be discouraged with
A world so full of sin,
For I can choose to live a life
That draws others to Him.

-Carol Hopson

Since this book has been all about trusting God in the difficult times, I was reminded of sitting beside my dear mother in church and listening to her beautiful voice sing hymns like "'Tis So Sweet to Trust in Jesus." At a very early age, I learned all the verses to some of the most precious hymns ever written, and I have always cherished the truths they taught me. Just recently I learned the story behind the writing of this wonderful hymn.

One day Louisa Stead (1850-1917), with her husband and four-year-old daughter, went to enjoy the beach at Long Island, New York. While there, they heard a call for help from a young child in the water. Mr. Stead went to his rescue, but instead, both he and the child were drowned. Louisa and her daughter were left to experience the pain of poverty and loss, but they continued to trust God. One day, after finding that some food and money had been left on her doorstep, she wrote the hymn "'Tis So Sweet to Trust in Jesus." Later, Louisa and her daughter left for South Africa where God provided a wonderful new husband, and they spent the rest of their lives serving the Lord as missionaries.

'Tis so sweet to trust in Jesus,
Just to take Him at His word,
Just to rest upon His promise,
Just to know, "Thus saith the Lord."

O how sweet to trust in Jesus,
Just to trust His cleansing blood,
Just in simple faith to plunge me
'Neath the healing, cleansing flood!

Yes, 'tis sweet to trust in Jesus,
Just from sin and self to cease,
Just from Jesus simply taking,
Life and rest and joy and peace.

I'm so glad I learned to trust Thee,
Precious Jesus, Savior, Friend;
And I know that Thou art with me,
Wilt be with me to the end.

Jesus, Jesus, how I trust Him!
How I've proved Him o'er and o'er!
Jesus, Jesus, precious Jesus!
O for grace to trust Him more!

You see, whether the problem is large or small, the answer is still the same...trust God in the process, and He will honor you, give you His peace, and use you for His glory. What could be better? *"May the God of hope fill you with all joy and peace in believing, that you may abound in hope by the power of the Holy Spirit"* (Romans 15:13).

Twenty Ways I Can Be Obedient and Trust God in These Troubling Times

(Written on October 20, 2008)

1. I can live by faith and not by sight, which honors the Lord (Hebrews 11:6).

2. I can choose to let God totally control my thoughts, words, and actions (Psalm 19:14; Colosians 3:17).

3. I can show kindness to those I disagree with (Ephesians 4:32, 1 John 4:7).

4. I can be a light to those who are lost (Matthew 5:16, 44).

5. I can choose to encourage those who are depressed and discouraged (Hebrews 10:25).

6. I can stay in God's Word daily for my peace and direction (Psalm 119:25-32).

7. I can remember that God has overcome the world (John 17:33).

8. I can pray more and trust more because of our nation's direction (1 Corinthians 15:58).

9. I can take comfort in the fact that God is near to the brokenhearted (Psalm 34:18).

10. I can trust God with the difficult and seemingly impossible (2 Chronicles 20:15-17).

11. I can be willing to forgive those who offend me

(Ephesians 4:32).

12. I can believe and trust that all things will work together for good (Romans 8:28).

13. I can choose to be holy in my behavior no matter what the circumstances are (1 Peter 1:15-16).

14. I can put my faith in the power of God and not in the wisdom of men (1 Corinthians 2:5).

15. I can prove the validity of my faith, which brings glory to God (1 Peter 1:6-7).

16. I can boast about my weaknesses that God's power will be seen in me (2 Corinthians 12:9-10).

17. I can remember that God is the stability of our times, not men (Isaiah 33:5-6).

18. I can be willing to possibly suffer for Christ in this world because of my beliefs (1 Peter 4:12-16).

19. I can rest in the knowledge that God will be triumphant (1 Corinthians 2:14; 15:57).

20. I can more eagerly anticipate the joy of spending eternity with Jesus (John 14:1-3).

To contact Carol for speaking engagements or to order additional copies of

Trusting God in Troubled Times

Go to her Web site at:

www.carolhopson.com

Or write her at

Carol Hopson
1015 Olive Crest Drive
Encinitas, CA 92024

E-mail: carolhopson@gmail.com

Other books by Carol Hopson include:

But God, This Wasn't My Plan

But God, I'm Tired of Waiting

Peace in the Midst

My Day, His Way

Hope and Help for a Mother's Heart

A New Song

Above the Storm

The Journey From Feelings to Faith